YOUR COMPLETE GUIDE TO EQUINE ARENAS

How to Build and Maintain an Ideal Riding
and Training Space—from the Ground Up

ABIGAIL BOATWRIGHT

TRAFALGAR SQUARE
North Pomfret, Vermont

First published in 2024 by
Trafalgar Square Books
North Pomfret, Vermont 05053

Copyright © 2024 Abigail Boatwright

All rights reserved. No part of this book may be reproduced, by any means, without written permission of the publisher, except by a reviewer quoting brief excerpts for a review in a magazine, newspaper, or website.

Disclaimer of Liability
The author and publisher shall have neither liability nor responsibility to any person or entity with respect to any loss or damage caused or alleged to be caused directly or indirectly by the information contained in this book. While the book is as accurate as the author can make it, there may be errors, omissions, and inaccuracies.

Trafalgar Square Books encourages the use of approved safety helmets in all equestrian sports and activities.

Trafalgar Square Books certifies that the content in this book was generated by a human expert on the subject, and the content was edited, fact-checked, and proofread by human publishing specialists with a lifetime of equestrian knowledge. TSB does not publish books generated by artificial intelligence (AI).

Library of Congress Cataloging-in-Publication Data
Names: Boatwright, Abigail, author.
Title: Your complete guide to equine arenas : how to build and maintain an ideal riding and training space—from the ground up / Abigail Boatwright.
Description: North Pomfret, Vermont : Trafalgar Square Books, 2024. | Includes bibliographical references and index.
Identifiers: LCCN 2023043536 (print) | LCCN 2023043537 (ebook) | ISBN 9781646011704 (hardcover) |
  ISBN 9781646011711 (epub)
Subjects: LCSH: Horse racing. | Race horses. | Thoroughbred horse.
Classification: LCC SF334 B63 2024 (print) | LCC SF334 (ebook) | DDC 798.4--dc23/eng/20231127
LC record available at https://lccn.loc.gov/2023043536
LC ebook record available at https://lccn.loc.gov/2023043537

All photographs by Abigail Boatwright *except* I.3 courtesy Mick Peterson; I.4 from Racing Surfaces White paper. Original by J. Thomason; 1.4, 1.7, 1.10 courtesy of Danny Austin; Maven Photos & Film; 2.1, 2.2, 3.3, 3.4, 7.2 Attwood Equestrian Surfaces; 6.1 Kate Bradley Byars; 6.2 A & B Arena Werks; 6.4 A & B courtesy Carolina Arena Equipment; 7.1 A & B sketches by Bob Kiser; 9.1 courtesy of Keeneland Photos; 9.2 courtesy of Michael "Mick" Peterson; 9.9, 9.10, 9.11 by Benoit Photo

Book design by Lauryl Eddlemon
Index by Andrea Jones (JonesLiteraryServices.com)
Cover design by RM Didier

Printed in China

10 9 8 7 6 5 4 3 2 1

For our horses,
who give us their hearts as we pursue our dreams.

CONTENTS

Foreword	vii
Author's Note	ix
Contributors	x

Introduction — 1
- Ideal Footing vs. Poor Footing — 3
- Footing Considerations — 5

Chapter 1: Planning Your Arena — 9
- Start with a Master Plan — 9
- Budget — 10
- Property Location — 15
- Usage — 23
- Size — 26
- Gates and Fencing — 29
- Lighting — 31
- Additional Amenities to Consider — 32

Chapter 2: Indoor vs. Outdoor — 41
- Indoor, Outdoor, or Covered? — 41
  - *Indoor and Covered Special Considerations* — 45
  - *Outdoor Special Considerations* — 46
- Cost Comparison — 49

Chapter 3: Footing — 52
- Attributes of an Arena Surface and Key Definitions — 52
- Choosing Arena Footing Materials — 56
- Finding Surface Materials and Creating the Right Footing Blend — 66
- Determining the Quality of Your Material — 69
- Footing Takeaway — 70

Chapter 4: Building an Arena — 74
- Beginning at the Bottom — 74
- Construction Steps — 77
  - *Outdoor Arena—English Disciplines: Step by Step* — 77
  - *Outdoor Arena—Western Disciplines: Step by Step* — 82
- Covered or Indoor Arena: Step by Step — 86
- Building Your Building Team — 90
- Your Responsibility — 92

Chapter 5: Moisture Management — 93
- The Right Amount of Moisture — 93
- Methods of Adding Moisture — 97
- Finding the Right Moisture Balance — 106
- Moisture Needs Vary By Discipline — 110
- Time of Year and Climate — 114
- Watering Routine — 114

Chapter 6: Arena Maintenance Equipment — 115
- Choosing Equipment — 115
- Equipment Basics — 116
- Maintaining Your Equipment — 125

Chapter 7: Arena Grooming and Maintenance — 127
- Regular Maintenance Techniques — 128
- Primary Maintenance Routines — 133
- Arena Care Don'ts — 136
- Maintaining Arenas for Specific Disciplines — 139

Chapter 8: Repairing and Assessing Your Arena — 151
- Problems with Footing — 151
- Problems with the Base — 154
- Getting Arena Feedback — 156
- Other Common Arena Issues — 157
- Arena Assessment — 158
  - *Start with Unmaintained Footing* — 158
  - *Walk and Observe* — 159
  - *Pay Attention While Dragging* — 159
- Survey the Arena — 159
- Check Sand Gradations — 161
- Check Moisture Content — 162
- Check Over Maintenance Equipment — 163
- Evaluate Your Drag Patterns — 163

Chapter 9: Racetracks — 164
- The Goal for Track Surfaces — 164
- The Science of Strides — 166
- Racetrack Construction — 167
- Track Surface Materials — 168
- Primer Notes for Caring for Track Surfaces — 176
- Exercise Tracks — 180
- Testing and Managing Track Wear and Weather Impacts — 181

Source Notes and Commentary — 189
Acknowledgments — 191
Index — 193

FOREWORD

The science of arena footing has been my life's work for 30 years. When Abigail Boatwright first approached me to write an article series about building and caring for arena footing 12 years ago, I was skeptical of how she would manage it. This topic is really too dense for an article—even two. You could write an entire book about it and not cover everything, and I told her that. But we did put together those articles, and when she came back to me a decade later, wanting to write that book about arenas, I agreed to help.

I've seen a lot of evolution in the way we build arenas, and the way we care for them. From the machinery we use, to the techniques and equipment, arenas have come a long way since I started. But what hasn't changed is the overarching goal of providing a safe, consistent surface for horses to perform at their best. I am dedicated to this mission with each arena I build, each horse show footing we maintain, and every consultation with clients. Abigail shares this vision, and in this book has aimed to provide readers with as much information as possible, without overloading you with data and science that would be difficult to interpret as an average horse person.

Throughout this book, you'll find practical advice to help inform you as you work to build or maintain your own arena. Abigail has included vital information from my experience, as well as the knowledge of several other experts—many of whom I know and have worked with myself. While no book can replace the invaluable contribution of an expert builder, knowing what is needed for your arena and how to care for it will make you a better owner, trainer, and rider, and I believe will ultimately help your horse have a safer experience as your partner.

Best of luck.

Bob Kiser
Founder, Kiser Ranch Development
(Formerly Kiser Arena Specialists)

AUTHOR'S NOTE

The topic of arena footing is extensive, and whenever I've written a magazine article on the subject over the years, I've been amazed at how much important information I just couldn't include due to word count limitations. Every time, I thought to myself, *This subject could be a whole book.*

Well, I'm happy to share, *this* is that book.

I'm a lifetime horse enthusiast, and I've been an equine media journalist for 18 years. While I do not have the knowledge or expertise to write this book alone, I have collaborated with a number of experts at the top of their fields on every element in these pages (meet them next!). You can trust their expertise, and as I wrote this book, informed by their knowledge, I approached each chapter with the perspective of a horse owner. What would I want to know if I was building my own arena? What do I need to know to care for arena footing I already have? How can I tell if this ground will be good for my horse, as I ride in my sport of choice? This book is for everyone, from beginners who are just trying to find good ground where they can ride their horse, to professionals who want to design and maintain a high-end training or competitions space.

My goal for this book is to equip you with the knowledge to give your horse safe footing—regardless of what arena footing you're starting with, or what discipline you ride. I intend this book to help prepare you for all the factors you need to consider if you are planning to build an arena, including what options are available, what types of footing you can select, and what decisions you'll need to make as you work with a builder. If you are simply hoping to maintain or improve the arena you already have, you will learn the basics of how to care for arena footing—choosing equipment, grooming the footing to suit your chosen riding discipline, and repairing issues with your ground. I've also included a chapter on caring for racetracks, with insight from leading racetrack managers.

I know your time is valuable, and I thank you for spending it reading these pages. I wish you good ground for your horses, always!

Abigail Boatwright

CONTRIBUTORS

A very special thank you to each of these experts for generously allowing recorded interviews and giving their time and knowledge to help me write this book. **Your Complete Guide to Equine Arenas** would not have been possible without their expertise.

Bob Kiser is the founder of Kiser Arena Specialists, recently rebranded to Kiser Ranch Development, and is considered the foremost expert on Western arena construction and maintenance. Kiser has been maintaining the footing at the National Reining Horse Futurity in Oklahoma City, Oklahoma, since 1986, and maintains the footing at the NRHA Derby as well. Kiser and his son, Jim Kiser, have been involved in building arenas in 42 states and 10 countries. The company has managed arena footing for the National Reined Cow Horse Association Futurity and National Cutting Horse Association Futurities, and the American Quarter Horse Association World Championship Show for more than 20 years. Kiser provided the footing and equipment for reining events at four different World Equestrian Games competitions and The American Professional Horseman. The company continues to manage the footing and provide arena drags for AQHA, NRHA, NCHA, and NRCHA major events.

Nick Attwood is the founder of Attwood Equestrian Surfaces, which is the official footing and arena company of US Equestrian. Attwood builds arenas for jumping, eventing, and dressage riders, and tracks and gallops, as well as major horse show facilities such as Morven Park in Virginia, Stable View in South Carolina, Virginia Horse Center in Virginia, Great Meadow in Virginia, Windurra USA in Pennsylvania, and Fair Hill in Maryland—a five-star event that is FEI-sanctioned.

Randy Snodgress owned Snodgress Equipment, the creator of Arena Werks™ rotating harrow arena maintenance equipment. Arena Werks is the official drag of the Appaloosa Nationals and Appaloosa World Show, the Cactus Reining Classic, the High Roller Reining Classic, the NSBA World Championship Show, The Paint Horse Congress, the APHA World Championship Show, the Pinto Color Breed Congress, the Ranch Sorting National Championship, Reining by the Bay, The Run For A Million, the Stock Horse Of Texas World Show, and other events. Snodgress is based in Joshua, Texas, just outside Fort Worth.

Danny Austin owns Austin Arena Specialists, a full-service equine facility consulting, planning, and construction company. He is based in Southern California and has been the arena specialist caring for five-star FEI events, including the Longines Los Angeles Masters.

Leland Smith maintains the footing for several major barrel races held at the Lazy E Arena in Guthrie, Oklahoma, including the Heartland Tour and Barrel Bash. He has more than 20 years' experience maintaining barrel and rodeo ground, and has been a horse trainer for three decades.

Roby Roberts is the co-owner of World Equestrian Center in Wilmington, Ohio, and Ocala, Florida. He built the facility with his wife, Jennie, and it opened in January 2021.

Vinnie Card is the director of operations at World Equestrian Center, Ocala.

Sydney Cannon is pursuing a master's degree at the University of Kentucky in biosystems and agricultural engineering. Her research project works with water trucks used at racetracks. She also works at the racing surfaces testing lab managed by Mick Peterson (see right column).

David Detweiler owns Carolina Arena Company in Abbeville, South Carolina. His equipment, including the DragNfly and DragNfly Pro, have been used at many bigger English horse show facilities such as the World Equestrian Center in Ocala, Florida; Palm Beach International Equestrian Center in West Palm Beach, Florida; Tryon International Equestrian Center in Mill Spring, North Carolina; Greater Southwest Center in Katy, Texas; the World Equestrian Games; and the South American Games.

Randy Spraggins has installed and maintained the footing at major rodeo events, including the Wrangler® National Finals Rodeo (WNFR). He handled the stadium conversion at Globe Life Field in Arlington, Texas, for the 2020 WNFR, the PBR Tour around the United States, and The American Rodeo at Globe Life Field. He has nearly 40 years' experience.

Mick Peterson, Ph.D is the director of the Racetrack Safety Program, and a professor of biosystems and agricultural engineering at the University of Kentucky. He is the executive director of the Racing Services Testing Laboratory. His research has focused on the biomechanics of animals and how they respond to various properties in surfaces. His work includes ultrasonic imaging and a wide range of data collection and testing, which has been used to create quality control protocols to improve racing surfaces.

George McDermott was the track superintendent at Lone Star Park in Grand Prairie, Texas, for seven years. He was at Louisiana Downs in Bossier City for 30 years and the track superintendent for 15 of them. He was a temporary track manager at Beula Park in Grove City, Ohio, to train track crews. He has also been a consultant for many different racetracks.

Steve Wood is the assistant track manager at Del Mar Racetrack in Del Mar, California. As soon as Steve Wood was able to work, he was involved on the "backside," helping his dad maintain surfaces at various tracks. When he turned 18, he started working at California tracks Del Mar, Santa Anita, and Pomona. He has helped his dad build training facilities and horse arenas. Today he works with track superintendent Dennis Moore to maintain Del Mar's track.

Jim Pendergest graduated from the University of Kentucky with a degree in animal science and has worked at and managed Thoroughbred breeding and racing farms. He then managed the Thoroughbred stock at Kentucky Training Center in Lexington, and went on to maintain the track at the facility. He has been managing the racing surfaces at the service center for over 30 years. Churchill Downs bought the center, and then Keeneland bought it two years later. Pendergest has been working for Keeneland since 2000. He has also managed a Keeneland-owned company that made polytrack and oversaw installations at 14 racetracks around the country before the business closed in 2011. Since 2019, he has managed the Kentucky Training Center and has been the Director of Racing Surfaces for Keeneland's turf track, dirt track, and polytrack training track.

INTRODUCTION

Spoiler alert: you do not need an arena to ride your horse.

Wait, don't close the book just yet! It's true, though—you can ride your horse perfectly well in a flat pasture, on the trail, or on a grassy roadside shoulder. Horses are supremely suited to handle tough terrain. Thank goodness.

But if you want to pursue training goals with your horse, if you want to compete in horse shows, or you plan to ask your horse to perform athletic maneuvers at speeds faster than a walk or trot, you'll probably want to ride in a designated area with consistent footing. Grass is often uneven, it can get worn down, and it can get slick or muddy when it rains. So at some point, just about all of us will be riding in an arena with some kind of commercial footing.

Footing in competition arenas has evolved significantly over the last century. Bob Kiser is the founder of Kiser Ranch Development. His family has competed in reining horse competitions from 1978 to present, and he recalls many occasions where his horses would come home sore after a competition. (His experience includes harness tracks, in addition to a wide array of competition footings and surfaces.)

"You could hear those horses galloping for a quarter mile!" Kiser says with a laugh. "But nobody thought much about it. That's the way it was. Used to be, you talked to a roper about the ground, and he'd say, 'As long as it doesn't have cactus growing in it, I'll be all right.'"

Good footing is crucial to reducing short- and long-term injury to your horse's limbs and joints. It also keeps you both safer, as your horse is less likely to trip or fall on consistent footing. And it allows your horse to perform at his highest potential. But good ground doesn't happen by accident. A random patch of dirt is not likely the best footing for your horse.

Your horse's soundness doesn't solely depend on how "good" the arena footing is. There are many factors, including: genetics, conformation, temperament,

I.1 An ideal riding surface is consistent and offers sufficient support in order to prevent injury and assist in optimal performance in the horse.

speed, fitness level, and overall conditioning. All these play a vital role in your horse's soundness in addition to the arena footing. When you're working with a horse for years to achieve training goals, good footing plays a key part in the process. Poor footing can derail that progress at any point.

"The footing is so important, especially with dressage horses," Nick Attwood, founder of Attwood Equestrian Surfaces, says. "It's really important for the longevity and health of the horse to have good footing. Otherwise, the horse may not be able to get to the higher levels, because they might have gotten injured before that point."

Ideal Footing vs. Poor Footing

The Fédération Équestre Internationale (the International Federation for Equestrian Sports or FEI) has published an extensive article titled "Equine Surfaces White Paper," and the paper describes the two elements that contribute to most injuries in the horse during equestrian sports.

- *Intrinsic factors* include anatomical characteristics and physiological functions, as well as your horse's temperament. These affect the way your horse's body tissue responds to exercise, and his predisposition to orthopedic injuries.

- *Extrinsic factors* interact with these intrinsic factors to affect your horse's performance ability, and his susceptibility to injuries. Extrinsic factors include

I.2 Your horse's soundness doesn't solely depend on how "good" the arena footing is—many factors have influence, including your horse's genetics, conformation, the way he moves, his temperament, his physical fitness, conditioning, and health care.

I.3 Good footing is crucial to reducing short, and long-term injury to your horse's limbs and joints. It also keeps you and your horse safer, as your horse is less likely to trip or fall on consistent surfaces.

the amount, intensity, and type of training; and health care, stabling conditions, and surfaces on which your horse trains.

Your arena footing is an important factor that can either contribute to injuries or reduce them. While there is no one perfect surface for every purpose, there are several surfaces that can work well for different uses (I'll highlight these in chapter 3—p. 56).

An ideal surface for safety and performance includes:

- Consistency of footing.
- Sufficient support to the horse.
- Properties that aid in the horse's maneuvers.

On the other side of the coin, studies have found that, on hard surfaces, for example, there is an increase the likelihood of bone and joint-related injury in horses' lower limbs. This is partly because of high frequency vibrations and concussive forces from the hooves impacting the ground. Show jumpers competing on hard ground have especially suffered from front-foot soreness and concussive injuries.

Footing Considerations

Stride and Loading

Consider figure I.4 on this page. According to *Equestrian Surfaces, a Guide*, a book published by the Swedish Equestrian Federation and translated into

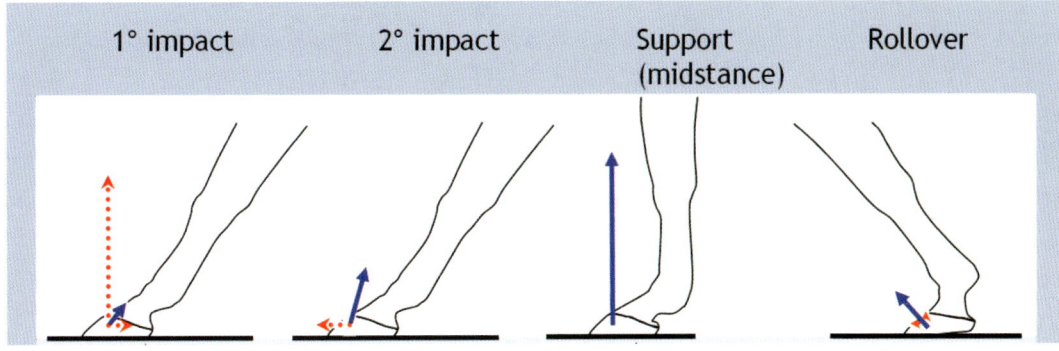

I.4 A stride is measured from the moment a hoof touches the ground, until it touches the ground again in the horse's next step. Here you see the hoof-surface interaction from left to right: landing, full contact, loading, and rollover.

English by the FEI, a *stride* is measured from the moment a hoof touches the ground, until it touches the ground again in the horse's next step. This includes a *support phase*, when the hoof is on the ground, and a *swing phase*, when the hoof is in the air. While the hoof is on the ground, a typical horse hoof-surface interaction looks like this:

Hoof Landing ➔ Full Contact ➔ Load ➔ Rollover

> ## PHASES OF THE HOOF-SURFACE INTERACTION
>
> - **Hoof Landing:** The horse's hoof has hit the ground and stopped.
> - **Full Contact:** The whole hoof is touching the ground.
> - **Load:** The hoof touching the ground is carrying the full weight of the horse.
> - **Rollover:** Moving into the next stride, the hoof leaves the ground. This starts with the heel and "rolls over" the toe last.

A horse experiences loading on his limb vertically and horizontally, as well as motion that is both rotational and sliding. The surface on which your horse is landing plays a key role in how the hoof and limb responds during this sequence.

Variation In Training Is Desirable

It's not necessary for your horse to work on a perfectly consistent footing every single time he's being ridden. In *Equestrian Surfaces, training variation* is defined as "riding on a variety of surfaces. This includes using more than one arena, but especially riding on varied natural terrain (quiet) roads and riding paths."

Your horse's body adapts to the surface on which he's being ridden. If you ride on the same surface, prepared the same way, every time, your horse's musculoskeletal system may not be prepared for potential variations in footing out on the trail or when traveling to other arenas for competition, and it could increase his risk of injury.

Performance vs. Injury Prevention

A surface that provides the best performance does not always mean it's the best for reducing injuries. If the footing allows your horse to move at speed and make fast turns, it may not offer as much shock

RIDING ARENA MYTH-BUSTING

Myth: A perfect arena is possible.
Truth: It's impossible to achieve a "perfect" arena footing. Nick Attwood of Attwood Equestrian Surfaces says there are many philosophies of how to build and maintain arenas, and each arena is a series of compromises. There's no single way to build an arena.

Myth: The better an arena footing is, the easier it is to maintain.
Truth: Although it may seem counterintuitive, a well-constructed arena is not maintenance-free. "The best arenas often need more maintenance," Attwood says. "There's a tradeoff from the get-go." He says some of his clients are surprised at how much maintenance an arena requires, even one that is high-end with the very best blend of materials. "If you have footing with sand and textiles, for example, but you don't maintain it regularly and keep it moist, then the sand and textiles will unincorporate. The textiles will literally come to the surface, and it becomes a problem. Spending a lot of money on your arena can make the footing better, but it's often going to be more work."

If you choose a sand blend that needs to be watered, then it requires more maintenance, watering, and harrowing. If you choose a polymer-coated surface like Pinnacle, it will be less maintenance because it does not need to be watered (see more about this in chapter 3—p. 62).

Myth: An outdoor arena needs to be "crowned" around the perimeter.
Truth: Attwood says this is a disaster design flaw and it creates more problems than it solves. A "crown" slopes from a raised center down to the edges. As you drag and ride on this type of design, the footing material will migrate down the slope. Eventually there will be an uneven layer of material throughout the arena, with no footing at the center, and far more footing around the perimeter. Instead of crowning, "You should just make it all slope in one direction," Attwood says. "It's best to slope toward one side."

Myth: All you need for a good arena surface is a good drag.
Truth: Randy Snodgress, owner of Arena Werks drag equipment, says it's a misconception that any arena can be fixed up with a good piece of drag equipment. Just having the implement does not make for good ground. Protocols such as varying your drag patterns and dragging correctly are vital to improving your ground (see more about this in chapter 7—p. 129).

absorption for your horse's legs as an arena with footing that allows for more shear movement but less "grip."

Nick Attwood says equestrians are aiming for a surface that is somewhere between being *too hard* and *too loose*. You're also looking for a degree of "grippiness," while also allowing for the hoof to slide about half an inch after hitting the ground. The "rebound property" of the ground is also important to performance.

Our experts suggest that variables such as manure content, moisture levels, and dust created are key to determining if footing is ideal or poor. We will discuss each of these topics, and many more, in the coming chapters.

By the end of this book, you will be armed with information needed to make decisions for your own arena, whether it's building from scratch, improving on what you have or maintaining what's already there. You will also know when it would be best to consult a professional at each step of the way.

• CHAPTER 1 •
PLANNING YOUR ARENA

Let's say you have the means and the space to build your "dream arena." Before you begin, it's wise to take some time to carefully plan for the process. An arena is an expensive project, no matter the size, so you'll want to consider several points before you start so you can (hopefully) avoid making costly or time-consuming mistakes.

Start with a Master Plan

Nick Attwood recommends putting together a *master plan* for your arena project before commencing with construction. Attwood says of about a half-dozen experts he knows who specialize in arenas and riding facilities, all of them begin with a detailed plan outlining the project.

"The master plan has all the details: orientation of the arena, where the barn, paddocks, and arenas are [on the property]," Attwood says. "If you're going to

1.1 Your master plan should consider all needs and variables for your situation now, and the future, before you break ground.

expand, you want to be thinking about that before you even start. Plan where the expansions will go, too."

(Note that everything that follows is only touched upon briefly here for consideration in a master plan; I expand upon each subject in the chapters ahead.)

Budget

This is the biggest deciding factor. You're going to be making a significant investment, and the amount you can spend determines much of what you'll be able to do.

> ### QUICK REFERENCE:
> ### Arena Build Terminology
>
> **Pad Site:** The physical location for your arena.
>
> **Base:** The bottom layer of your arena. It offers stability.
>
> **Middle Layer:** Sometimes referred to as a "sub-surface." The segment of material between the base and top layer. Not all arenas have a middle layer.
>
> **Top Layer:** The top few inches of material in an arena (sometimes called "top dressing"), which should be stable and consistent across the arena.

"If you're thinking about building an arena from scratch, the budget is everything," Attwood says. "For us at Attwood Equestrian Surfaces to build a 100- by 200-foot arena with everything 'standard,' by the time you've finished, you're looking at a couple hundred thousand dollars—if you want a really good arena. That's the Pinnacle [footing]. And not everyone can afford that. So you have to make compromises about what the end result will be."

Budgetary Considerations

In order to start putting together your budget, ask yourself the following questions:

- Will you be hiring contractors, or will you be doing some of the work yourself?

- What size arena do you want, and what is the cost of building in those dimensions?

- Will your arena be outdoor? Indoor? Covered?

- What features will be included? Lighting? Fans? Seating? Sound system? Sprinklers?

- What material will be used for the footing? Is it local, or will it need to be shipped in?

- What method will you use to add moisture, and how much does it cost?

I.2 An indoor or covered round pen is built similarly to a regular indoor arena, but its smaller area can mean lowered building costs.

- What equipment will you use to maintain the footing, and how much does it cost?
- How will you maintain the arena? Will you manage it yourself or hire help?
- Will it be a trainer's headquarters, with dozens of horses using it, seven days a week? Will you host horse shows with different events there? Or will it be used a couple of times a week by one rider?
- Are riders performing reining maneuvers, jumping courses, or running speed events every day, or are there less demanding forms of recreation?
- Will this be the only arena on the property, or will there be more than one area to ride?
- Will you be riding in the arena year-round, or are there times of the year where it'll get more use over others?

The answers to these questions will help inform your budget. How? Here are a few examples:

Size Reduction: One of the best ways to cut costs is not by cutting corners, but in reducing the size of your arena.

"If you can be happy with a smaller arena, you can probably increase the quality of what you build," Attwood says. "Everything is about how much the costs are per square foot. If budget is a real consideration, spend a little more on getting quality footing and being able to take care of it."

A smaller arena also means you'll be able to build a sprinkler system that more effectively saturates the entire arena, should you choose that method of moisture management. Attwood says an arena that is 100 feet wide needs large sprinkler heads that can spray 50 to 70 feet, which are more expensive than regular sprinkler heads that shoot water 30 feet. (Find more on various watering methods in chapter 5—p. 93.)

Footing and Watering Systems: If you invest in footing that doesn't need to be watered, you'll spend more money up front, but you won't need to invest in watering equipment or the time to water the arena and wipe down dust.

"A footing that we call 'plain vanilla,' which is sand and textiles, it can be about $4 a square foot, but if you buy footing that doesn't require any watering [such as wax or polymer-coated sand—see chapter 3 for more info] that's going to be double, maybe even three times the amount, but you'll save on the cost of water and time watering," Attwood

1.3 The location of your arena on your property influences costs significantly. Choose a spot where you do not have to fight Mother Nature to build and maintain your riding pad, which may add substantial cost.

says. "If water is expensive where you are, then you need to think about going with a footing that doesn't need watering, or an efficient watering system that's going to maximize the water that you put into the footing."

For example, Wolfgang Bacher, owner of Bacher Products and expert in equestrian surfaces, installed an underground watering system that uses far less water than a sprinkler system in an arena for actor Clint Eastwood in the Los Angeles area. "Putting in that watering system reduced his watering bill from $50,000 a month to $20,000," Attwood says.

Danny Austin, owner of Austin Arena Specialists, advises his clients to invest in the best they can on footing, put a good fence up, and then add fans and other features like windscreens down the road. "Those are things you can do as the budget allows you, as time goes on," Austin says. "But you can't really cut corners on your base or your footing. Once those are put down, you can't really upgrade. They need to be done at the beginning."

"If you want your horses sound, and you want your arena to work, first and foremost you need to focus on your base footing layer," he says. "And then everything else should fall in line, depending on your discipline."

Drainage: If you're installing a drainage system between a base and top layer, that will increase the overall cost, but can enhance the arena's usability during a rainy season.

Material Sources: Where you source materials has a huge impact on your costs. In some instances, materials can be found locally, ensuring transportation costs are minimal.

"I've got an arena right here in Whitesboro, Texas, that we didn't have to import anything—we built everything with the materials that were right there on the property," Austin says. "It was literally, take the grass off, stockpile the material that we knew we could use for the base and footing, grade the pad, then lay everything back down in layers to make the base and footing out of it."

The result was a beautiful arena—one that would cost someone 20 miles down the road $200,000, Austin says. This arena—turnkey—was $40,000.

"Your soil type drastically changes the budget," Austin says. "As does the topography of the land. If we have something that is very gentle sloping—that's going to take very little earthwork, and will keep the costs down. The less dirt has to move, the less material trucked in, the less cost."

If you are building an arena that is not close to

where materials are sourced, you'll pay much more in transportation costs, increasing your overall expense. "Logistics play a huge role today," Austin says. "Trucking didn't used to be such a big deal, but trucking costs are so much higher than they were 20 years ago."

If you're shopping for property and know you'll want to build an arena, it's wise to consider where you will be sourcing your footing and building materials when thinking about costs.

"Before you buy a piece of property, it's always good to evaluate the site, and if there's a better option [closer to materials or more suited to an arena without as much earthwork] still in the same region, entertain that, because if could save you a ton of money on the project," Austin says.

Indoor vs. Outdoor: In Attwood's experience, an indoor arena's actual footing is less expensive to install than an outdoor's because the base and construction is simple, and you won't need a costly drainage system. Outdoor arenas, you'll need to plan for drainage and containment, which ups the cost.

Attwood builds a lot of high-end arenas, which can cost several hundred thousand dollars. He says being realistic about your budget is the best decision you can make for your arena.

OVERBUILD

Whenever your budget allows, *overbuild*, particularly on the quality of your footing.

"Don't ever cut corners, the corners will just come back and haunt you forever," Austin says. "You might save 10 percent on construction, but if you were trying to save on say, drainage, then you didn't actually save, and you'll actually lose due to shut down time for those several weeks while the arena dries out from a freak weather storm."

While you can go cheaper on fencing or a gate, it is best to avoid scrimping on base material, footing, grading, drainage and diverting water around your place.

Property Location

Where you locate your arena on your property depends on several factors. Convenience for riders is important, but Austin says prioritizing easy accessibility over a suitable site is a mistake.

"Sometimes the function comes before the form," Austin says. "A lot of times the best location may not be the best location for you to ride. Let's say you want an arena 50 feet from your barn. It is so critical to

I.4 Your property's terrain will impact where a quality arena can be built and successfully maintained.

figure out all the drainage, make sure it will work in that location, and think about how the weather will affect it, not just convenience."

Consider what distance from the barn would be best for your situation—you don't want it so close that dust from the arena coats the stalls and horses, or where horses in the barn distract horses in the arena. But you also don't want to locate the arena so far from the barn that it's inconvenient or time-consuming to walk back and forth for each horse being worked. You also need to plan for how you'll access water for sprinklers or your water trailer.

"About 100 yards is a good distance," Attwood recommends.

If you're building your entire equine facility from scratch, Austin says you ideally want to start by situating your arena at the best possible location, and then choosing where your barn will go. "It is so much easier to build a barn in a less-than-ideal location than it is to build an arena on an unsuitable site," he says.

If you're planning an outdoor arena, the soil type at the pad site is very important. Austin recommends testing the soil of your potential arena location before making further plans. This can look like taking an excavator or an auger for drilling fence posts, and drilling several holes to see what the soil composition is. Do you have rock just below the surface? Clay? Water? Having this information in hand before planning further can save you money and headaches.

"If you're trying to stay within a budget, placing that arena is the first thing you want to place before anything else," Austin says. "I like to lay out the arena, then I design where the barn, round pen and other buildings are going to fit into the layout. And then my road system that carries throughout the property. But as a whole, where an arena fits into a project, in my opinion, should be the priority."

Where you put your arena on your property has budgetary considerations, Austin says. Choosing a location where you have to fight Mother Nature to build and maintain an arena can add $40,000 to $150,000 more to your overall costs.

"You can move your location over say, 100 feet, and suddenly it can be $50,000, $60,000 more just in earthwork," Austin says. "This comes from time, fuel, equipment, and other costs."

Be sure to consider:

Terrain: The terrain at the spot where you want to build affects the cost of building tremendously. "If it's hilly, you've got to move some dirt to get a level pad from which to start," Attwood says. "Just moving dirt turns out to be quite expensive. So if you can, you want to try to minimize that."

Orientation: How the arena lays out north, south, east, and west—is another consideration. For example, if you're a dressage rider, and you want to put mirrors at one end of your outdoor arena, you'll want to orient the arena with the long sides running north to south to avoid being blinded by the sun coming up. "You spend more time going down the long ways, and if you ride in the morning, or in the evening, you don't want the sun in your eyes," Attwood says.

Proximity to Roads and Traffic: Building an outdoor or covered arena too close to a road can increase distractions for horses and riders.

ROUND PEN TIPS

An indoor or covered round pen is built similarly to a regular indoor arena (I discuss the indoor versus outdoor question in the next chapter—see p. 41). An outdoor round pen, however, is a different story, especially when made for Western disciplines. An arena using synthetic footing and a drainage system can withstand tremendous rain and be ready to ride on in hours, whereas a round pen made with traditional materials such as sand, silt, and clay cannot. Drainage is critical in a round pen, Austin says.

"We drain them like an umbrella—there's a high point in the center, and they drain all 360 degrees, so they slope like an umbrella to sheet water," Austin says. "We don't want to stop up water. We have to divert any water that flows onto them, and we have to get it to flow off."

Austin says avoiding runoff and water pathways when you're planning a round pen is even more important than with a full-size arena.

"So many times I see people have let outside water run through an arena," Austin says. "The arena should only have to drain what water is actually falling on it. It should not have to deal with any outside water. And this is even more of a big deal for a round pen."

Aim to keep your round pen high and dry. Austin sometimes builds a round pen on top of fine crushed limestone instead of the clay base used in an indoor pen, to encourage better drainage.

Attwood says an outdoor round pen can be challenging to maintain because of the drainage issues. Another

Proximity to Trees: Building near a tree line can offer shade for an outdoor pen, but it can also increase chances of issues with root systems. Attwood says a good rule of thumb is to understand that the root system of a tree spreads at least as far as the tree's canopy.

"We've done quite a few arenas where people

1.5 A & B When building round pens, proper drainage is even more critical than for an arena. Aim to keep your outdoor round pen high and dry, without waterways flowing through during rainstorms, or cover it, like these examples.

method is to have the outer edges higher than the center—like a NASCAR track—but with a drainage hole in the center.

"That way when it rains, the water has a way of going down the center—perhaps it's a hole full of drain rock," Attwood says. "And at the bottom, there's another pipe that diverts water to somewhere away from the arena."

For a hot walker space—where horses circle either tethered or within panels for exercise, Austin says to avoid a slick base—make sure it still has traction.

"Round pen footing, for a pen that has a roof over it, is more like good cow-horse footing," Austin says.

A round pen can be difficult to maintain because maintenance equipment needs to be able to fit through the gate, and dragging a round pen footing all the way to the edges is a struggle.

Planning Your Arena | 19

have a tree that they've not wanted to take down, and we've incorporated it into the arena," Attwood says. "But the way you incorporate it, you can't have the footing come right up to the trunk."

Deciduous trees also introduce leaves, flowers, and seeds, which can be inconvenient when they fall into the arena because you'll want to remove them—you don't want the composition of the footing changed by the accidental addition of organic material. And removing tree detritus by picking or blowing them off the arena surface takes time.

Regional Climate and Environmental Conditions: The region where your arena is located affects how it is built and maintained. Attwood says some areas of the United States, like North and South Carolina have sandy, loamy ground (more explanation of this type of ground in chapter 3—see p. 58), but it can lead to instability when building on it.

"We've built arenas in South Carolina, and the first thing we did after stripping off the top soil was to bring in between a foot and 18 inches of super stable dirt," Attwood says. "In South Carolina, they called it 'sand clay.' It's a mixture of sand and clay. When you put a layer 12 to 18 inches deep down below your footing, it becomes almost like a concrete pad to start from."

Water Patterns: You need to know how water naturally flows on your property, to avoid putting your arena in the middle of a runoff path.

"The idea is to try not to disrupt Mother Nature too much," Austin says. "The least impact we have, and the more natural we keep it, the better it is for everything. Less impact on the budget, the property, and you want to preserve the water's natural course of flow."

Attwood advises against placing your arena in a low spot on your property—you want to avoid putting it in a "bowl." Even with drainage installed, this can cause issues with your arena.

"You don't want all the water from the surrounding fields ending up around your arena, because that becomes a problem if you build an arena with drainage," Attwood says. "That drainage needs to be for the water captured on top of the arena, and it needs to drain out and go somewhere. So the arena needs to be higher than the place where the water is going to drain toward."

To find out the water patterns on your property, particularly drainage and runoff, you want to look at the *sheet flow water*, which is your surface water. You can get this information from a topographical survey of your property with the elevations and the water flow clearly shown.

1.6 When selecting an arena location, pay attention to the water patterns on your property to avoid water flow issues where you plan to ride and train.

"Somebody with a really good eye can walk out on a piece of property and can see whether it's wet or dry," Austin says, "If you're budget-minded and just want to figure it out on your own, go out to your property right at the end of a heavy rainstorm and see where your soft spots are. See where water is running. Water will show you where it runs—downhill, through ditches, whatever it needs to do to drain."

If you are researching a place to buy, Austin says don't be fooled by how the property looks on a sunny day. "The worst time—when it's very wet—may be the best time to evaluate the arena site," Austin says. "Don't wait till it's a beautiful day; go when the weather is awful and it's rained for three weeks. Then you can see where those low water areas are."

Also be sure to check your legal survey, as areas designated as "wetlands" on the property you are considering may be marked, and it may be unlawful to change the topography or build on or near that area.

Testing Is Imperative

When time is of the essence and your budget is tight, you might think it makes sense to skip testing your arena area and drilling test holes in the grading site before beginning construction. But Austin says building an arena without the crucial pieces of information gleaned from testing can end up causing further delays and expenses if you eventually find your arena site is unsuitable or unusable. This can be due to water flow or other issues.

"I like to core 10 to 15 feet, so we normally have a company come out and dig test cores throughout the grading site," Austin says. "They can tell you what the soil is like and if they encounter groundwater. It might cost you $2,500 in exploration, but it could save you thousands and thousands."

Attwood says testing soil at a potential arena location will help you determine how far down you'd need to go before you hit bedrock, a harder base, or other changes in the soil composition. In constructing an arena, you remove a top layer of grass and organic material, so this research helps you know how far down you need to dig. Attwood performs this exploration with a mini excavator, or even digs holes with a shovel. Regardless, the information gained is vital in planning.

"Let's say you had a paddock or pasture and there was grass on topsoil, and then you constructed an arena on top," Attwood says. "All that organic material—the roots and the grass—it dies, it decomposes, and then that layer becomes really unstable. Then you can run into a problem where the arena layers [on top] collapse in different areas."

Usage

The way you build your arena should be influenced by how you plan to use it. The disciplines performing on the footing make a difference in both the type of footing (more in chapter 3—p. 93) and maintenance (more in chapter 8—p. 151) of your ground. For example, with an arena primarily used by reiners, Austin may start with a clay base. If it is a covered arena that will probably be used by no more than 10 to 12 horses per day, he can install a thinner base layer—perhaps 4 or 5 inches. For a professional trainer's arena that could see 50 to 60 horses a day, Austin would double the depth of the base, putting in 7 or 8 inches of clay.

"We know that the arena is going to need maintenance later, and that gives us more room to do [so] in say, 5 to 10 years," Austin says. "In a Western arena, for more horses and more impact, you're going to want a stronger, thicker base layer."

These days, the indoor arenas Austin builds are very specialized by discipline. An arena footing built for all-around Western events, such as Western pleasure, is not going to be ideal for reining without a lot of maintenance to change the properties of the ground.

"We have a basic footing mix that we do that is similar to reining ground, but it has more 'hold' to it," Austin says. "So it's not quite as quick—the base is not as hard as a clay base or as defined as a reining base."

An arena for all-around riding will not only have less depth to its footing, it will also be a shallower arena than, say, a cow-horse arena, which needs deeper footing with more hold. An arena for barrel racing, too, has to have a deeper base and footing that grips together. Attwood says jumpers prefer a firmer footing, while dressage riders want slightly less firm footing with a little more rebound. An eventer does both of the latter disciplines, so wants to find a happy medium.

"It used to be, it was a one-size-fits-all scenario, but as the industry's changed, it's getting to where

> **QUICK REFERENCE:**
> **Arena Build Terminology**
>
> **Rebound:** The footing or material surface's ability to return to its natural state after a horse's footfalls.
>
> **Grip:** The amount of sliding—horizontal movement—the horse's hoof does during landing, turning, and pushing off (sometimes referred to as "hold").

we're tuning arenas for exact disciplines now," Austin says.

If you're a multi-discipline barn, there will have to be tradeoffs for riders, but a good footing mix *can* work for more than one sport. Attwood says the needed minor changes can be made with good maintenance.

"In a good arena, if the formula is done correctly, you can manipulate it to get the properties you want," Attwood says. "If you're jumping horses once or twice a week, and perhaps you're doing flatwork and dressage the other days, you can build the arena to where you just need to add more moisture to it to 'tighten it up' for jumping, and then when it dries out a little bit, it's more suitable for flatwork and dressage."

EXERCISE TRACK TIPS

An exercise track—a straight line, oval, or circle that is typically 20 feet (6 meters) wide, and varying distance or length—can be helpful for a variety of uses when training horses, but they're most often used for conditioning, particularly racehorses.

Attwood says the topography of the area where the track will be located is important. "Many trainers want the horses [they are conditioning] to be able to go uphill—it can be a useful training technique, and builds strength in the back of the horse."

Building a track on a slope can be challenging for drainage though. Footing can get washed down the hill. Attwood says including proper drainage in your base underneath the footing can minimize this issue.

Kiser says the only way to avoid losing your footing this way is to slope no more than 1 percent. (See more about track building and maintenance in chapter 9—p. 164.)

Think About the Future

Plan for future use of your arena, if possible, Austin says.

"I get so many people who say, 'Oh, I'm barely going to use it.' Next thing they've added on another 50 stalls, and got another trainer in there, and the arena was built for 20 horses a day, but you have 90 horses a day on it," says Austin. "Then they're calling me because the arena isn't holding up."

Shows vs. Training

Attwood says building an arena designed to be used for horse shows, and an arena at a training facility, are two different scenarios.

"For horse shows, the footing is typically a little bit firmer than for training," Attwood says.

1.7 Your primary discipline and estimated horse traffic will help you decide how to design your riding arena.

When you have multiple disciplines in the same arena, firmer is the best choice for all, rather than softer. Firmer is more versatile.

Horses tend to perform better on firmer arenas, Kiser says, but everyday training is harder on horses' legs in those arenas.

If you're building an arena that needs to be used every day, and you have 25 horses that need to be exercised, Attwood says you need to make sure the arena is built as correctly as you can afford.

"You have to have the right amount of drainage, and the right system that makes it easy to water it," Attwood says.

Size

A 100- by 200-foot arena is a good size for most Western disciplines, Austin says. Some reiners with big training operations prefer 150- by 300-feet or bigger to handle more riders at one time and to accommodate longer straight rundowns. Barrel racing arena maintenance expert Leland Smith suggests an ideal arena for this event should be about 150 to 200 feet long, with a minimum of 120 feet wide to leave 15 feet on each side of the barrel on a standard barrel course before you get to the fence.

The thing to consider is the exponential cost when making an arena bigger than you might need.

"It just gets out of hand real quick," Austin says. "100 by 200 feet is 20,000 square feet. If someone wants to make it a bit bigger, such as 150 by 300 feet, what they don't realize is that's 45,000 square feet. That is more than double the size. It doesn't look like it or sound like it until you figure up the square footage."

Ideal Arena Dimensions by Discipline

DISCIPLINE	DIMENSIONS
Western and English All-Purpose	100 x 200 feet (30 x 60 meters)
Reining	150 x 300 feet (45 x 90 meters) or bigger
Barrel Racing	150 x 200 feet (45 x 60 meters); minimum 120 feet (37 meters) wide
Dressage	Standard: 66 x 197 feet (20 x 60 meters) Small: 66 x 132 feet (20 x 40 meters)
Jumping	100 x 200 feet (30 x 60 meters), up to 100 x 230 feet (30 x 70 meters)

I.8 When planning the size of a covered arena, consider the actual riding space, which will be smaller than the dimensions of the exterior supports by several feet.

Alternatively, if you are building a covered arena, consider the size you may eventually need, because modifying those dimensions is difficult after the arena is finished. Austin says at minimum, start with the maximum width you need and as close to the length as possible.

"If you're going to build a covered pen, don't build a 100 by 200 [feet] if you know you'll need one that is 150 by 300—there's no extending the width," Austin says. "If you can only afford to go 150 by 200, and you'd really like to have 150 by 300, build a 150 by 200, because you can possibly add 100 feet of length onto the building if you have to."

And think about space needs beyond the dimensions required for training. For example, while a regulation dressage ring is 20 meters wide and 60 meters

Planning Your Arena | 27

I.9 The dimensions of a standard-size dressage arena are 20 by 60 meters (66 by 197 feet), but most riders require additional footage beyond the ring's perimeter fence.

long (66 by 197 feet), there is also the "small" option that is 20 by 40 meters (66 by 132 feet). But whichever size you choose, most riders will want the arena to be larger than the actual dressage ring.

"Many dressage riders want to build an arena where they can put a dressage fence in the center and have 10 feet all the way around it on the outside so they can ride around the outside and then come into the 'ring,'" Attwood says. "So a large dressage arena is 20 by 60 meters, which is essentially 66 by 197 feet, but we'll end up adding 20 feet to that on both dimensions."

A classic jumping arena size is 100 by 200 feet, but Attwood says some riders want it to be longer—more like 230 feet long.

"This allows them to recreate combinations that are often seen at a horse show," Attwood says. "And if you're going to have three separate jumps all the way down one side [a triple combination, for example], you really need about 230 feet to achieve that."

From Attwood's perspective, whatever your discipline and usage, the bigger you can build your arena, the better for longevity purposes. "Make it as big as you can afford," he says.

A smaller arena, especially an indoor arena, will see more wear on the outer perimeter due to lack of room.

"Those arenas become quite difficult to take care of because a track develops where the horses are being ridden all the time," Attwood says. "And a smaller arena wears out quicker. The footing eventually becomes inconsistent."

Gates and Fencing

Gate Location

Most Western arenas are designed in a simple rectangle shape. Where you put the gate depends on the arena's orientation to your barn or other buildings, but you also want to consider how you'll be dragging the arena.

"I like to enter an arena [to drag] either on a center or a corner of the short side," Austin says. "The main reason is for your tractor drag. When you're on your final pattern and you want to exit the gate, you want to not have to diagonally cut across the arena. It keeps your drag pattern clean."

This may sound like overthinking the situation, but if you have to drag your arena multiple times a day, the extra time needed to cross back over your drag pattern to get to a gate in an awkward spot can be inconvenient.

Dragging aside, some riders and certain disciplines simply prefer to walk through a gate situated in the center or a corner of the short end versus the long side.

Fencing or Walls

Most arenas Attwood builds have a method of "containment"—he compares it to the sides of a sandbox. This consists of 4-by-4-inch posts placed every 4 feet. Inside of those posts are 2-by-12-inch pressure treated boards, extending a foot up from the ground to make a barrier. This barrier can be extended 3 or 4 feet high as a fence. Everything else for the arena is built inside that perimeter. Fencing materials can include lumber, plastic, or metal. They can have spaces or be solid. If wood fencing or walls will be exposed to the weather, Bob Kiser says it should be creosote-treated to keep it from rotting. (Note, however, Austin does not prefer this.) Some regions may use hardwoods, such as white oak, or a softer wood like yellow pine tongue-and-groove. Some facilities may opt for a pipe fence line with just the bottom 10 to 12 inches made of pressure-treated boards to "hold in" the arena footing in that "sandbox" scenario.

Attwood installs indoor arenas with slanted or curved *kick walls* (or *kickboards*). Often when you're building an indoor arena, the trusses supporting the roof may jut out from the walls. Attwood says a kick wall or fence can "smooth out the edges." You have the choice of simple plywood, a fence line, or a slanted kick wall. That kick wall can extend above the eye line of the horse to reduce distractions, or be another height according to preference.

"It's basically a safety device," Attwood says. "A kick wall can keep your legs from bashing into the wall. We make curved plywood panels that you can put in an indoor arena. They're most often used for dressage, and they look beautiful."

Austin says most Western arenas have a vertical fence rather than a curved kick wall, anywhere from 4 to 6 feet high. If it's a cow horse arena, you could see the fence 5½ to 6 feet high.

"A steel welded fence or wood-and-steel

TWO WESTERN SPORTS, TWO DIFFERENT ARENA FENCES

Austin says reining horse riders may not need to invest in the same kind of fence as say, a cow-horse rider.

"Cow-horse people want to make sure they've got a great fence so that when they are working a cow down the fence, or push a cow into a corner, that fence is going to hold," Austin says. "The reiner is not so worried about that because they're not working on the fence. A reiner's budget needs to be more focused on the actual footing, base system, and quality of the surface, and the fence is of lesser importance."

combination is most common," Austin says.

When thinking about the desired dimensions of your arena that you would like to include a kick wall or interior fence, you need to consider how much of the building will be lost to the space it takes up.

"The further inward your fence or kick wall extends from the building, the more space in the building you're going to lose," Attwood says. "But with something like metal trusses [for roof support], if you put the fence too close to it because you want to save space, your head could be 6 inches from the metal truss as you ride around the outside edge of your arena. That is a safety concern."

Lighting

Think about the time of day you're planning to ride—will you want to ride early in the morning or at night? If so, you'll need lights. What kind depends on how you'll use the ring or pen.

I.10 A–C *Three kinds of arena perimeter "barriers": Outdoor arenas can have no fence, or have fences made of wood, PVC, metal piping, or wire, among other materials. (A). When the trusses or support beams impose on the arena's perimeter, as they do in Photo B, a kick wall will give you more riding room and keep horses and riders safe. When you work cattle in an arena, a solid fence—as opposed to one with gaps—helps keep your cattle flowing and stops them from "locking up" (C).*

I.11 A & B **When you plan to ride at night, you'll need proper lighting (A). Fans are an important feature for arenas in warm climates, as they help cool and increase the comfort level for both horse and rider (B); however, when trying to keep costs low on a new arena build, focus on footing and fencing first, and add amenities like fans when your budget allows.**

"Do you need perfect light for what you're doing—stadium lighting—or do you just want to be able to lope circles at night?" Austin asks. "That needs to be factored in to your budget and put in order of priority."

Lighting has evolved dramatically over the last several decades, thanks to the invention of LED lights. Older lights used to take 10 minutes to reach full brightness. LED high-bay lights are much more energy efficient.

"You can run an entire 150-by-300-foot arena on what it used to take to run two halogen bulbs," Austin says. "The actual light isn't cheap, but it cuts back on your electricity draw tremendously."

Additional Amenities to Consider

In a covered arena, you may want to look at adding fans and windscreens. Those who compete in certain disciplines, including dressage and reining Freestyles, may want a method to play and hear music. Some riders like to include mirrors on the wall or fence line. These little "add-ons" can take up a significant chunk of your budget.

If you will likely have spectators visiting your arena, you may want to invest in a viewing area. While this can be fairly easy to accommodate around an outdoor or covered arena, Attwood says for an indoor arena, you'll need to factor in 1,000 to 2,000 square feet of the building's overall floorspace for people to watch from beyond the arena perimeter.

Getting Good Advice

The most important thing to know about improving your arena, or planning to build a new one, is that you certainly don't have to do it all yourself. It is highly recommended you get help. Kiser says reputable arena consultants have a lot of experience with different types of arenas and footing. You should reach out to an arena consultant with a reputation for building arenas for your chosen discipline. Unfortunately, these types of experts can be hard to find, and the good ones are often overwhelmed with projects.

Start with a good arena and work backward. Is there an arena in your area that you feel works well in the all the basic areas we just touched on? Austin says research arenas, talk to trainers, ride in spaces nearby (always ask how an arena holds up after it rains). Once you've found an arena you could see yourself riding in—find out who the builder was.

"See if you can get that builder to come out and look at your site," Austin says. "That's way better than asking around on social media."

Attwood says if someone you know has a nice arena that has good footing, consider replicating some elements for your own facility. But it's still wise to consult an arena expert—*not* a builder—before jumping into the project, for both your own budget and your horse's sake.

When you've found someone who does great work, Austin says to be patient—they may be busy because they deliver excellent results.

"If you can get a good earthwork guy who's willing to come out and do some consulting, help you put some rough budget numbers together, that can give you an idea," Austin says. "Is the grading going to be $50,000, or $100,000 for this particular site? They'll be able to help you."

Make sure your expert is truly an expert. Austin says avoid relying on a real estate agent, or a horse trainer, when planning a site for your future arena. And don't only look at the builders of brand-new arenas. Ask for references from clients with arenas that are already five or six years old.

Attwood suggests getting a consultation from someone who has built a number of arenas—the experience gained on each new project is invaluable.

CASE STUDY

WORLD EQUESTRIAN CENTER

Located in Ocala, Florida, the World Equestrian Center (WEC) opened in 2021. It is one of the premier equestrian centers in the world, hosting world-class equestrian competitions across many disciplines, including international-level show jumping and dressage along with various hunter, breed, and driving events. The 700-plus acre facility has 22 outdoor arenas and 5 climate-controlled indoor arenas.

Planning

Mary Roberts and the late Ralph "Larry" Roberts Sr. built the flagship World Equestrian Center in Wilmington, Ohio, 30 years ago. When their son Roby and his wife Jennie planned for a new center in Ocala, they desired to build a facility to be a place to encourage youth equine enthusiasts and bring families together, as well as share their faith.

"It's all about family, and bringing kids together, and our goal has always been to try to be all-inclusive," Roby says. "We try to make it for everyone from the beginner to the person who's very advanced, that has made it, from jumping the top Grand Prix course in the country, to the person who just wants to lease a horse for a weekend."

The Roberts are horse enthusiasts themselves, with a background with Quarter Horses. Their daughter turned toward hunter-jumper riding, and continued through youth competition on into breeding hunter-jumper horses herself.

Before beginning a building project—even if it's not as large as WEC, Roby recommends developing a vision for your completed project.

"One of the things that sets us apart is that we're a business built on and driven on values," Roby says. "Even down to the construction materials—we poured the floor so that horse's wouldn't slip. All the stalls have 'stable mattresses,' which are more comfortable for the equine athletes. We have 6,000 security cameras and a 24-hour security team because we want people to feel safe here. It's very time-consuming, but we love that it changes people's lives for the better."

I.12 *The main ring and Equestrian Hotel at the World Equestrian Center in Ocala, Florida.*

I.13 The entryway at the World Equestrian Center in Ocala, Florida.

WEC's director of operations Vinnie Card says when you're planning your facility, consider what you want to do on the grounds.

"If you want to host local horse shows, there are plenty of things you might want to have, such as a pavilion, or a shade structure near the arena for people to stand under and watch the horses warm up and practice," Vinnie says. "Or if you're selling horses, make sure you have proper equipment around when you're going to start to jump in the arena or train your horses."

Building Process

The WEC facility is located on 6,000 acres in central Florida—much larger than the Wilmington, Ohio, facility's several hundred acres. In addition to its more than 400,000 square feet of indoor riding space, and five large outdoor arenas, WEC Ocala has

2,100 permanent stalls that are climate-controlled, along with another 800 temporary stalls. The site includes The Equestrian Hotel, seven restaurants, convention space, shopping opportunities and more. The dog-friendly Riding Academy Hotel complex was completed in 2024, which includes more than 400 rooms, a convention and retail center, and five dining concepts.

Building the center began in 2016, and the majority of the work wrapped up before COVID-19 hit the world in 2020. Fortunately, WEC did not suffer from the rampant supply chain issues, and construction was complete before opening in January 2021.

"We just had to have a really good plan, and we went at it from all different angles," Roby says. "We missed some construction dates, and we fast-forwarded other ones. We just started with a plan, pecked away at it, and built on our plan. It got a little bigger and we added more as we went."

The facility took on a bit of a life of its own, Roby says. It evolved into what it's supposed to be. For example, because Ocala did not have enough infrastructure to support the sewer and water needs of WEC, the Roberts had to build a water plant and a sewer plant.

The Facility

WEC Ocala hosts events ranging from a dog show to a small horse show with 100 entries to major events with 3,000 horses. Reiners, hunter-jumpers, dressage and Western dressage, and most major breeds have events there.

"It's not made just for one breed, it's made for all breeds," Roby says. "We always say that both of the facilities belong to everybody. Everybody that comes in and wants to be part of the sport, it's their place too."

The facility also has convention space to host gatherings of all interests, including home and garden shows, wine festivals, exotic car auctions, and more.

"With the size of the place, and we're constantly increasing the size of it and buildings, we're not limited to just one thing," Roby says. "We're unlimited to do multiple things."

A Focus on Safety

Each outdoor arena is surrounded by live oak trees and have pavilions adjacent, and restrooms nearby. Each arena is bordered by white wooden fences.

Safety is a priority, Vinnie says. "Our biggest concern is knowing how horses are, when they see something new, they want to go the other way," he emphasizes. "So in a lot of our arenas, we try to keep everyday traffic like golf carts, dirt bikes, bicycles and cars away from the arenas. Most of our rings are in secluded areas, with rubber footing in the holding areas."

The footing inside the arenas is forgiving, Vinnie says. Rider feedback has said the horses like the sand/fiber mix, and they have a good feel under their feet.

"They feel really content and safe with their riders directing them around the course," Vinnie says.

WEC Ocala has been constructed to withstand a Category 4 hurricane, and includes climate control. The arenas are built around a huge courtyard, with the main ring in the middle backed by a hotel. The arenas are outfitted with powerful lights to illuminate the space. The result of this design is a beautiful space that makes it easy to observe horses in the arenas.

"Lighting is important—because you don't want to have shadows," Roby says. "Shadows can cause accidents."

I.14 A–D The 700-plus-acre WEC facility has 22 outdoor arenas and 5 climate-controlled indoor arenas, as well as almost 3,000 stalls.

Arena Footing and Maintenance

Footing is a priority at WEC, and Roby and Jennie both says it should be the number one thing for any facility. Discount Dirt Works installed all the arenas at WEC—starting with a base, drainage, up to the synthetic sand/fiber footing mix as the riding surface. And WEC has at least 12 arena specialists responsible for maintaining the arenas on a daily basis.

Reining and barrel racing require very different footing than the hunter-jumper events. So the arena that hosts Western shows contains footing that is suited to those sports—and the Roberts plan to build more in the future. That arena has a clay/sand mixture with no synthetics.

"It's a totally different thing because those reiners want to slide, and the barrel racers want it deep enough so they can get into it and turn really sharp," Vinnie says.

"Right now we just have one arena with reining and barrel footing, and all the other arenas have the hunter-jumper type footing, the fiber and sand mix," adds Roby.

The care of the outdoor arenas and moisture applied to the footing is based on changes with the weather, Vinnie says.

"It could be cloudy one day and you don't need as much water," he explains. "It could be sunny and hot and need twice as much water, especially if the wind is blowing and it's drying it out faster. But we try to maintain a certain moisture level in our footing in order for the riders and the horses to have the best quality landings and takeoffs and turning abilities to make it safe."

The facility's arena grooming equipment comes from Florida Coast Equipment and Reist Industries.

"They've been proven to do a really good job with what we're looking to accomplish, day in and day out," Vinnie says. "We have a full-time team here that does nothing but ground maintenance for us throughout the year for all the breeds and disciplines."

Maintenance starts early—4:30 or 5:00 a.m. during events—in order to prepare arenas before the show starts. The arenas are maintained throughout the day to keep the footing at the specs needed for the sports.

Once a week, Vinnie's maintenance crew selects two or three rings and laser-grades them, finishing with a good mixing of the footing.

Roby says to maintain a top-quality arena and facility, don't overlook the small things.

"I think you have to constantly maintain your footing as be a living, breathing thing," he says. "We just kind of do what we do and focus on what we do—and what everybody else does, they do. But I think our success has been because we look at the details."

• CHAPTER 2 •
INDOOR VS. OUTDOOR

When you compare an outdoor arena to an indoor, the building, maintenance, and use of that arena are very different. Both indoor and outdoor arenas have pros and cons, so before deciding to build, carefully consider which type best suits your needs and budget.

Nick Attwood says there are basically three kinds of arenas: *indoor, outdoor,* and *covered.* There are also combinations of the three, such as an arena that is enclosed at one end and uncovered at the other.

An *outdoor* arena has no roof or covering; an *indoor* is completely enclosed with walls and a roof; and a *covered* arena is a hybrid—it has a roof and support beams, but may have no walls. It might have a fence around the arena, or it may have half-walls, but no glassed-in windows. Attwood says covered arenas are most popular in warmer locations, where riders are looking for shade and rain cover, more than insulation from cold air.

An outdoor arena is more complicated, says Attwood, because you have to consider the weather and elements when building the footing. Construction of the building itself aside, building an indoor is easier when it comes to footing and the base—he says it's the least complicated of the three types.

Indoor, Outdoor, or Covered?

Danny Austin says climate is often a big deciding factor in the type of arena you choose to build.

"In my opinion, in North Texas [for example], I don't know how you could get a job done [training horses]—unless it was a small personal arena at home—without having a cover over it," Austin says. "We either have sun that cooks you to death, or we have rain and wind blowing on you."

If you live in a temperate climate with infrequent heavy rain—Southern California, for example—Austin says an outdoor arena can sometimes get by with a

TYPE	PROS	CONS
INDOOR	• Simple footing + base • Year-round riding regardless of weather • Controlled environment • Easier lighting setup • Climate control • Longer lifespan for footing • Can be repaired regardless of weather conditions	• Reduced ventilation • Can have inconsistent moisture • Higher initial cost
OUTDOOR	• Varied sensory experiences for your horse • Can be done on a smaller budget • Enjoyable experience riding in nature • Can be made larger for lower cost versus the same size of indoor	• Moisture inconsistency • More complicated footing/drainage/base • More powerful lights needed with stronger infrastructure • Footing will need to be replaced sooner • Weather can prevent year-round, consistent riding and training

less complicated base than needed elsewhere, and you'll be able to ride year-round.

Attwood says it's easier to maintain an indoor arena because it's less susceptible to weather-related changes. So if your area experiences heavy or frequent rain, extreme heat or cold or other weather conditions, an indoor arena makes sense.

"We build arenas in places like Minnesota, and there's no way you can train a horse outside in the winter there," he explains. "It's impossible."

Another consideration: Setting up lights in an indoor arena is easier than for an outdoor, says Austin. You don't have to install light poles—your lights can be ceiling mounted. And you can more easily avoid shadows because the lights can be scattered across the ceiling.

Depending on how an indoor arena is constructed, you may have areas in the arena that dry out faster than other spots. If a window or skylight shines on the footing, that area can dry out faster. In contrast,

2.1 An indoor or covered arena does not need the same type of complicated drainage system or base as an outdoor arena.

2.2 An outdoor arena can be made larger for less cost than an indoor arena—but climate will dictate its feasibility as a year-round training space.

an outdoor arena that has been properly built will dry out more evenly due to consistent sun and wind.

"A lot of covered arenas have skylights, or three or four fans, and that can dry the footing out," Austin says. "You have to make sure you have a good way to water them and keep them evenly watered."

If your indoor footing needs to be repaired or replaced, an indoor arena means your contractor can work anytime, regardless of weather conditions, Austin says. And indoor footing tends to hold up longer than outdoor.

"In a covered arena, Mother Nature is just not wreaking havoc on footing 24/7," he explains. "The surface of an indoor arena could last two or three times longer than an outdoor arena."

Generally, you won't have to water an indoor arena as often as an outdoor, which will save you money on water and time. An indoor arena also reduces the need for a complicated drainage system, which can save you a lot of the cost of building the base and footing.

"A lot of times if we put a roof over an arena, we'll save 40 to 50 percent of our cost of what we would have had to do with the base to make it strong enough if it was uncovered," Austin says. "So if you put a roof up, it saves a ton of money on the base. Does that offset the cost of the roof? No, it doesn't. But now you've got an arena that's going to last for a long time because it's not going to have to go through weather events. It's not getting rain, wind, or sun. And you're going to have way more riding time per year for that particular arena."

Austin says adding a cover to an arena adds to the overall cost about 15 to 20 percent. So, once climate is considered, it's a choice between spending money on your base, or money on a cover.

One benefit to an outdoor arena is the ability to expose your horse to more sensory input—especially helpful for training young horses.

"If you want to show your horses, train them to be desensitized to distracting things going on around the perimeter of an arena," Attwood says. But if you have a spooky horse, distractions in an outdoor arena can sometimes be a negative rather than a positive, he indicates.

"If you just have an indoor, they're kind of sheltered—you have windscreens, a solid fence, perfect lighting…but if you have an outdoor, you have wind blowing around, something could get blown across the property, birds, maybe a squirrel, more noise and exposure," Austin says. "To me, a horse gets a lot more broke if you have some outdoor riding time as well. In my opinion, it's great to have both if you can."

Indoor and Covered Special Considerations

Types of Structure
Attwood builds three main types of indoor arenas.

Wood-Beam Structure—This type is common in Europe and on the East Coast. From the Midwest eastward, Austin says many arenas are built with a wood beam structure. Attwood calls this a "pole barn," where the trusses are made of lumber sunk into concrete.

Metal Structure—From coast to coast, many indoor arenas have a steel structure cover. Attwood says some metal buildings have a frame made from engineered pieces in a pre-fab kit, set on concrete piers. The roof and siding can be sheet metal. You can add insulation, which can be helpful for horse and rider comfort, depending on your climate.

Fabric Structure—Another variation of a metal structure is similar to a tent. Attwood says this third type of arena has an aluminum frame covered with heavy-duty canvas. They may not look as attractive from the outside, but Attwood says they're very bright inside with a very high roof. (Roof height is an important consideration: The purpose of your arena may impact the height you need. For example, if you're planning to do any jumping, the roof needs to be a minimum of 12 feet tall.)

Size
An indoor arena needs to be at least 70 feet wide by 200 feet, Attwood says. This will allow space for a kickwall (see p. 30), while still giving you enough room to perform a 20-meter circle. If you are jumping in your indoor, it should be a minimum of 100 feet wide by ideally 230 feet.

As you make an indoor arena larger, the total cost rises exponentially. Attwood says adding to the length of an indoor arena costs less than adding to the width.

Ventilation
Air movement and proper ventilation in an indoor arena is important for the horse's health, and for the rider's comfort.

"Stagnant air is so uncomfortable in an indoor arena," Austin says. "It's like being in your car with the windows rolled up. It's like trying to work your horse in a sauna. I think it's crucial to have proper airflow, especially in climates where it can get 110 degrees outside."

Addressing decreased ventilation is a major challenge in an indoor arena, according to "Equine Surfaces White Paper." The amount of ventilation you have varies, depending on the type of covered arena you build. If you have a covered arena with open-air sides, you should naturally have good ventilation. But if you have solid fencing, walls, or windscreens, you may need to add other means to increase airflow.

"On a covered arena, you've got to watch how your wall or fence is constructed," Austin says. "A solid fence is great in the wintertime because it keeps some of that rain from blowing in sideways if you don't have windscreens. But in the summertime, it really cuts your airflow down. So you have to make sure you have fans."

Here are a few ways to improve ventilation in an indoor or covered arena:

Fans—You can easily add fans to an indoor arena—not only for ventilation purposes but to help keep you cooler on a hot day. Attwood says a fan can also help remove diesel fumes from your tractor. You can create airflow with *overhead fans* or *extractor fans*. Some fans have been built specifically for large areas, like Big Ass Fans or Macro Air. Look for a fan that is quiet, while still moving large amounts of air.

Ridge Vents and Cupolas—These allow hot air trapped in the roof to escape through the ridge of the building, Austin says. Cupolas are more often seen in barn roofs than arenas.

Removable Windscreens—Windscreens installed around the perimeter of an arena reduce strong winds coming into your arena, but they also reduce airflow. If your screens can be opened or removed, that can allow more ventilation.

Windows—You can select window panels that can be opened manually or with a motor. Attwood says many high-end indoor arenas include motor-operated windows that operate like garage doors, and they're a helpful feature.

Outdoor Special Considerations

Base and Footing

The greatest disadvantage to an outdoor arena is variations in moisture and temperature, says "Equine Surfaces White Paper." This makes keeping the surface consistent a continual challenge. As I've mentioned, an outdoor arena requires extensive attention to building a strong base and drainage system to handle rain and other weather elements.

When an outdoor arena has synthetic footing, or a wax coating, it can be negatively affected by extreme weather. And some footing can freeze solid in an outdoor arena when temperatures dip below freezing.

2.3 Covered and indoor arenas need methods of ventilation, such as the large overhead fan and open sides above the half-wall shown here.

Lighting

An outdoor arena needs lights similar to a football or baseball field, placed high enough and angled so they shine on the whole arena.

"Way more powerful lights are required [than indoors], way more infrastructure," Austin says. "You have to have underground cabling too. It's at least four times the cost to light an outdoor versus an indoor."

Fencing

Whether or not you put a fence around your outdoor arena depends on if you want the safety of

2.4 *An outdoor arena requires lighting similar to an athletic field. Lights are often placed on high poles and positioned to illuminate the entire riding surface.*

containment. Think about how you'll use the arena, Attwood says.

"If you're giving lessons to green riders, you'd be foolish not to put a 3-foot-6-inch fence all the way around the arena," he advises. "And if you want to keep other animals such as deer out of the arena, a fence is helpful."

Performance riders use the fence in an arena for many reasons. These include: dictating circle size, visualizing straight lines, utilizing corners for approaches to lines and obstacles, assisting in sliding stops and lateral work, and so forth.

"Some people don't put a fence at all, and other people will," Attwood says. "If it's just for aesthetics, you may put one that is 18 inches…just to beautify the space."

Attwood builds outdoor arena fences with three categories of materials.

Wood—This is the least expensive material. Wood is fully customizable for function and appearance.

PVC—This material is often white, but color options are available. Attwood says PVC fences don't look as aesthetically pleasing, but they require less maintenance than wood.

Metal—Typically steel or aluminum, metal fencing can be beautiful and lasts well. It is the most durable of the materials Attwood works with.

Cost Comparison

So which type of arena costs the most? It's not as clear cut as "indoor = more expensive." Austin says many folks don't consider extra costs when looking at building an outdoor pen or arena.

"I've got outdoor arenas I've built here in Texas in the last year that might range from $50,000 to $60,000, then I have outdoors that have been well over $400,000 in build," Austin says. "The whole thing is a package."

"Some horse folks choose to build an outdoor and cut corners, so that it's pretty darn good but may not be amazing. This allows them to ride outside most of the time, but they don't add lights, for example. They may go outside, have fun, and get a little training in with their horses, and then they come in and use the premium surface with the awesome lights to get all their 'big stuff' done."

This is why when you're going to spend a large amount of money for a top-notch outdoor arena, Austin says it might be worth considering the extra $12 to

2.5 Deciding between an indoor, covered, and outdoor arena, and which amenities you include, is dependent on the climate, your budget, and your preference for riding and training.

2.3 Riding time can be enjoyed both indoors and out. With the help of knowledgeable advisors, you can invest in the best scenario for both reaching your training and performance goals, and for the well-being of your horse.

$20 per square foot to add a roof, where you can stay dry and in the shade year-round.

"A top-quality professional outdoor arena can be as expensive or more than an indoor or a covered arena very quickly," he notes.

Attwood says, in his experience, outdoor arenas can potentially be built at a lower cost-point because quality buildings to house them can expensive; however, remember that constructing the arena base and surface itself is more complicated outdoors, and the base is more expensive, so the decision may not be that easy to make.

Whether you have a roof or not, you'll want to choose the right blend of footing for your arena. We'll discuss footing options in the next chapter.

CHAPTER 3
FOOTING

Grass surfaces have historically been used for horse training and competition arenas. However, with climate issues, year-round use, required maintenance, demanding performance maneuvers, and heightened injury risks, there's been an increase in the use and availability of synthetic surfaces. Grass is now *less* common for performance and professional arenas.

In absence of grass, most arenas are now comprised of mixtures of sand, silt, clay, and additives, such as woodchips, rubber, or fibers. Even though we're working with just a few ingredients, many factors can change how a footing material feels and behaves.

First, let's start by talking about the attributes of an arena surface and the terms we can use to describe their properties. Then, we'll talk about the advantages and disadvantages of these arena compositions.

Attributes of an Arena Surface and Key Definitions

Consistency is crucial to a good arena surface. While a horse can adapt to a range of surfaces, training on dramatically different surfaces may negatively impact performance and can be associated with injury.

There's a conundrum, though. Unlike surfaces designed for human athletics, an arena footing ideal for equine performance is not always ideal for long-term soundness, according to studies cited in "Equine Surfaces White Paper."

Footing for any equine sport should minimize concussion—of the hoof—through energy absorption, but still rebound power to aid performance. Here are a few terms and definitions used in the "Equine Surfaces White Paper" for reference as we continue the important discussion of footing:

3.1 *Grass footing allows for a small amount of sliding, but it's difficult to maintain and can be dangerously slippery when wet.*

Shock Absorption—This is either frictional and comes from particles being displaced, or structural, where shock absorption is achieved by compacting particles that will regain their shape. A surface's firmness against impact, and the amount of cushioning it has, determines how much a surface can absorb shock.

Shear Strength—When a hoof lands on a surface, the *shear strength* is the amount of resistance the footing can offer to keep the hoof from moving horizontally. This needs to be optimized for specific events—for example, barrel racing requires higher shear strength to avoid potential slipping. Shear strength depends on moisture content, temperature, and the composition of the arena material.

Hardness—This is how much resistance a material has against penetration with a defined object and a defined amount of pressure. It's difficult to measure *hardness* accurately on arena surfaces. It is related to *stiffness*—the ratio of applied force to deflection.

Response Time—The time between deformation of the surface when weight is added—a hoof landing—and the subsequent *elastic recovery*—a hoof leaving. If the elastic recovery occurs too quickly, increased force will be taken on by the horse's limbs.

Loss of Energy—When a hoof impacts a surface, some of the energy from the collision is lost. The amount depends on the elasticity of the surface's top layer.

Consistency—The *Oxford English Dictionary* defines consistency as "conforming to an unchanging pattern." When referring to arenas, we are talking about the consistency of the material around all areas of the arena, and from one point in time to another. Moisture content is the largest variable in footing's consistency. But inconsistent depth contributes the most to the risk of lameness, according to a study on dressage horses.

"An inconsistent surface will reduce the horse's confidence in the footing, and has been suggested as increasing the incidence of tripping and slipping and loss of balance (Murray et al, 2010a)," "Equine Surfaces" says.

Impact Firmness—This is the shock experienced by the horse and rider when the hoof contacts the surface. This relates to the hardness of the very top surfaces and its initial stiffness when your horse's hoof lands on it. Concrete has a very high impact firmness. When you put a thin layer of sand on top of concrete, you have far less impact firmness, while still having good support. When you place wood over wet clay, you have good impact firmness, while still having some cushion as the horse steps.

Cushioning—The supportiveness of a surface to the horse compared to how much "give" it has. You can also think of this as *force reduction*—how the layers of the footing absorb impact—when a hoof lands. A surface lacking good cushioning is stiff, or hard. One example of footing with good cushioning, but little elasticity, is a sandy beach with dry, deep sand.

Responsiveness—This is how "springy" the surface feels to the rider and the horse. Think of a trampoline. When you push downward because of your weight, it springs back and even bounces you upward. If the timing of the *rebound* matches the horse's movement, it will feel springy. If not, it will feel "dead" with no springiness to it. For example, a surface that is heavily compacted could rebound too quickly, which makes it feel stiff or dead.

Grip—The amount of sliding—horizontal movement—the horse's hoof does during landing, turning and pushing off. This comes from the interaction between the horse's hoof and the materials that interlock and hold the surface together. Friction on the top layer affects how your horse's hoof lands. You want a little bit of slide to help absorb the impact, but not so much that the surface is "slippery." Your horse needs to be able to push off the layer just below the surface. A high grip surface will stop your horse too quickly, while too little grip will allow him to slide too much.

Uniformity—How consistent the surface feels as the horse moves across it. An arena can look level, but the impact firmness, cushioning, responsiveness, and grip can still vary. Your horse can handle gradual changes across an arena, especially if they're visible. But sudden or wildly variant changes can cause your horse to trip or become injured.

Consistency Over Time—This refers to how much the surface changes with time and use. Sand can break down into smaller and smaller pieces, which turn into silt. Moisture changes can affect the grip, cushioning, and other factors as the arena dries out during a day. Horses working on the footing can alter consistency along the track and in other high traffic areas.

Surface Composition—Composition varies by region and discipline. For example, riders in the United Kingdom often use surfaces that are comprised of sand and rubber, sand and woodchip, and sand and polyvinylchloride (PVC). Common additives for dressage or jumping arenas include synthetic or natural fibers, rubber, and cloth or felt strips. A polymer or wax coating can also be applied to sand. This binds the footing material together and creates a hydrophobic—water-repellant—coating.

Choosing Arena Footing Materials

According to Bob Kiser, 90 percent of Western arenas use a combination of three primary classes of soil: sand, silt, and clay. Kiser says in nature, you'll never find pure samples of each—they will always be in some combination. This is a good thing. A small amount of clay will help bind pure sand together. What differentiates these three materials, Kiser explains, is their particle size. They can be purchased separately from each other, or as a mix.

"It is better to find material that is naturally the right mix," Kiser advises. "If you do mix them, you need to have the right equipment to do it, and only a very experienced arena builder is going to do it correctly."

3.2 Many English-discipline arenas use sand with additives to improve important elements of the footing. These may include fiber, rubber, cloth, or felt.

Sand

Most arena surfaces are largely comprised of a sand mix. Sand has the largest particle size of the three classes of soil. Sand itself has a variety of shapes and sizes, some natural, some manufactured from crushing rock. These variances affect the material's properties.

Our experts say the gradation of the material—how fine or coarse it is—along with the distribution of those grains of sand, are important.

"If the grains are all an identical size, that's a bit like a jar of marbles," Nick Attwood says. "Those marbles never really fit together very well. But when you pack round spheres into something, there's a maximum density that you can get."

Sand comes from rock, which has broken down into small pieces. *Beach sand* is very round and uniform in shape, which isn't optimal as it offers the horse poor grip.

"Beach sand is round because the way it was eroded over time is by a rolling action," Attwood says. "When beach sand is dry, it's incredibly hard to walk on. It has almost no support. That sand doesn't really work for horses. So that's why the gradation is really important."

Sand that is slightly more angular may hold together better. *Concrete sand*, typically used to make concrete, has a variety of particle sizes, but Kiser doesn't use concrete sand in blends of sand, silt, and clay because concrete sand tends to pack too tight and too hard to keep the consistency of good footing. Concrete sand also tends to be abrasive on the horse's hooves. Kiser says concrete sand can be a good choice for outdoor arenas when wind erosion is an issue.

Mason sand, which has been used in mortar for bricks, can be a little coarse, but Kiser uses it in some arenas. It is typically what is used for cutting horse arenas. When you want a sand that is slightly finer, ask for *cyclone* or *asphalt sand*.

In order to stabilize your sand, it will take 20 to 25 percent of a silt/clay combination to keep it usable up to 6 inches in depth. To increase durability, you can use sub-rounded sand with a high quartz content coated with wax.

Sand Pros

Readily available and inexpensive relative to other material options.

Sand Cons

Can be limited by what's available in your location. Sand-only footing will not work as an arena surface

> ## STEER CLEAR
>
> The sand variety known as *manufactured sand* is created when quarries break up bedrock into pieces, crushing it into a sand-like material. It is more angular and feels sharper. It holds together well but compacts more. This product is highly abrasive to your horse's feet. Due to this effect, Bob Kiser does not recommend manufactured sand in most arenas.

because it's too deep. Attwood says it's difficult to keep sand consistent in depth and moisture, particularly for English disciplines that require only about 2 inches of sand.

Sandy Loam

Sand and a mix of extremely decomposed organic material that has turned into the texture of silt gives you *sandy loam*.

Sandy Loam Pros

Kiser says sandy loam is the best material to use in an outdoor arena, particularly for reining, cow horse, or barrel horse events. It's commonly used in horse show arenas. This mixture sheds water easily and dries out quickly. When prepared well—smoothing the surface and eliminating slide tracks or hoofprints—water will flow off the surface of an outdoor arena without soaking in when the footing is compacted.

Sandy Loam Cons

If you get sandy loam topsoil that has black clay mixed in, Kiser says it's worthless as an arena footing material because it will simply turn to mud. When using sandy loam, be aware it requires quite a bit of water, due to its dusty nature.

"The silt in the loam is what makes it dusty," Kiser says (see sidebar). "Nobody wants it to be that dusty... so be prepared to water the arena more than you would with pure sand."

Rubber

This surface, used primarily in English disciplines, consists of sand and a form of rubber additive. The rubber portion is either a "crumb" consisting of particles 2 to 5 millimeters in diameter, or rubber pieces 25 to 40 millimeters in diameter. These rubber crumbs are put on top of a rolled sand subsurface (middle layer). It should not be used in outdoor arenas because it is lighter than sand and will float away during heavy rains, Kiser warns.

SILT AND CLAY COMPONENTS

Silt is the "middle" particle size on the scale of sand, silt, and clay. It is never used alone, as it gets too hard and dusty, Kiser says. It can be used in combination at about 15 percent clay and 15 percent silt when mixed with sand.

Clay is made up of the finest particles, compared to sand and silt. It works well as a base, as long as the *plasticity index*—ability to be shaped and molded—is above "12," and the arena is indoors.

The rubber used in footing can be new, but it is often made from recycled shredded carpet backing, tubing, processed tires or belting rubber. Of these sources, the FEI white paper "Equestrian Surfaces" says tire rubber is preferred due to availability and cost. Some arenas are made entirely of shredded rubber, but this is less common, says Attwood.

Rubber Pros
Rubber reduces compaction of the sand or woodchip surface, because it compresses with little change in volume while opening pores in the surface when pressure is applied, says "Equestrian Surfaces." Rubber products may also be cheaper than a premium sand-based surface.

Rubber Cons
If routine maintenance is neglected, there's an increase of the risk of injury on a woodchip and rubber surface.

The FEI white paper cites several studies that show runoff from an arena with newer (less than six months' old) rubber from tires as an additive can leach pollutants into nearby waterways. Be cognizant of where water drains from an arena with this composition, and consider "aging" rubber additives before adding them to your arena.

Wood
Many arena surfaces around the world incorporate wood chips or sawdust into sand. In arenas located in the northwestern United States and southern Canada, it is coined as 'hog fuel." (Kiser advises against using wood in Western performance arenas where sliding and quick turns are necessary.)

Use more durable woods, such as oak, versus pine. Wood chips the size of match sticks are ideal. These chips are mixed with a fine natural sand, which has a low percentage (5 percent) of filler. The wood should be about 30 percent of the overall blend.

A woodchip layer below the primary surface of an arena offers great cushioning by reducing hardness and increasing shock absorbency.

Wood Pros
This biodegradable renewable resource is both easy to attain and safe to dispose of. Wood adds responsiveness and elasticity to a surface, while stabilizing sand—when combined with the right type. It is also cheaper to install a wood/sand blend than a fiber/sand mixture.

"Equestrian Surfaces" says a wood blend is not ideal for the highest levels of competition, but with good maintenance, it can be used for many kinds of training and lower-level competition.

Wood Cons

Wood blends can get slippery when manure is present, and it needs to be replaced sooner than some other surface materials, such as sand and fiber. Depending on the type of wood, you may need to replace the top layer of a sand-and-wood mixture every three to five years. A sawdust mixture may need to be topped up every year. Wood products rubbing against sand also create more dust.

When using wood chips as a primary source material, there can be an increase in the occurrence of slipping in the horse. As wood materials degrade, there is a decrease in cushioning and shock absorption.

SAY "NO" TO MANURE

No matter what type of arena footing you choose, manure is detrimental to that surface. For example, in a sand-wood mixture, manure turns wood into a compost-like material, and when present below the top surface, it makes the footing slippery. And manure and urine will negatively affect a wax-coated sand footing, and can shorten the lifespan of a fiber-sand mixture footing.

Fiber and Felt

Some footing material additives include synthetic or natural fibers. Depending on your location, this could include natural or recycled materials, such as carpet scraps. Arena surfaces have included fiber and textile materials for over 20 years. Attwood says some arenas consist of 4 or 5 inches of sand and fiber.

The higher proportion of fiber, the more grip your horse will have. Attwood usually mixes 2 to 3 percent fiber in with a sand footing.

"If you've got 100 tons of sand, you need 2 to 3 tons of textiles," he says.

The ratio of fiber to felt is important. Attwood says if you have sand that needs to be "tightened up" for jumping, you'll want to add more fiber. If the sand is already tight and compact, you can use more felt and less fiber.

Ideally, you'll mix fiber with a fine, clean sand with little filler, because it'll adhere better to the fiber than a coarser sand. Fiber length ranges from ¼-inch up to 2 inches long. The pieces of felt are often about 1 inch square.

When maintaining a fiber/felt mixture, make sure it's well-mixed, properly watered, and harrowed, and that manure is removed. Do not allow the sand/fiber mixture to fully dry out, because this can cause an accumulation of fibers on the top

3.3 Adding natural fibers to sand, as seen in this footing, increases elastic recovery from impact, enhances durability, and requires less maintenance.

surface. You'll then have to water, and carefully remix the fiber and sand.

Fiber Pros
Adding natural fibers increases the elastic recovery from impact, while reducing compaction. When mixed with a sand-based surface, fiber can create a root-like structure, enhancing durability and drainage. It increases the support for the horse, with less maintenance and easier drainage.

Attwood says blending textiles such as felt and fiber into the sand knits the sand together, stopping the grains from moving and the surface from becoming too deep.

"Once you've got the formula right—sand and fiber—the depth of the footing plays a much less critical role in how it feels to the horse," Attwood says. "You can have 3 inches, 4 inches, 6 inches or 8 inches—you could have 2 feet—it's all knitted together, and the horse will still be able to move on the surface because it's a three-dimensional structure that is being held together."

Textiles make a sand footing firmer and tighter,

3.4 When using a fiber additive in your footing, the source is important. You want uniform fibers and a correct felt-to-fiber ratio.

Footing | 61

but it also stops the grains from compacting and getting too close to each other, preventing the footing from becoming too firm.

"You're making it tighter, but you're not making it harder," Attwood says, "You're adding a little bit of bounce to it because the fibers are allowing there to be air in the footing. Polyester fibers and felt add a bit of shock absorption, because sand by itself is 'dead.'"

Attwood says a mixture of sand, the right length and thickness of fiber and felt, the correct amount of water, and the right amount of air mixed into the footing by dragging, are the keys to a good riding surface.

"Once you get that combination of those five ingredients, and you've dragged it perfectly so you've put some air into it, then now you have essentially a surface that's as good as it gets," Attwood says. "It's relatively not that expensive. But maintaining it is going to be the thing."

Fiber Cons

Good-quality fiber can be more expensive than scrap fiber. The source of your fiber and felt is important. Attwood says in the past, people added random scraps, such as chopped up tennis shoes.

"What's evolved over the last 20 years, is companies have been specifically making the kind of textiles that you can blend with sand to give you a better footing," Attwood says. "The ingredients are better, they're more reproducible, and they're a lot more durable. You can still buy scrap… but the problem is you never know what you're getting."

Custom textiles have a uniform, ideal fiber length and felt-to-fiber ratio. Scrap, which is cheaper, often has an unknown fiber length, so it's less consistent.

Coated Sand

Wax used to coat sand surfaces include paraffin and microcrystalline. Kiser applies a proprietary blend of vegetable oil to sand.

Attwood says a wax or polymer coating on sand eliminates the need for adding water to the surface because it replicates how properly watered sand behaves. Polymer-coated footing also increases elasticity.

"If you take dry sand and add a soft wax to it, those grains of sand stick together," Attwood explains. "And that's good."

Coated Sand Pros

There are many good things about this footing material: less maintenance, no dust, more consistency across the surface, and a longer-lasting surface. One study found a wax-coated sand footing reduced incidence of lameness and injury, as compared to sand and wood-chip surfaces.

3.5 Textiles make a sand footing firmer and tighter, but also stop the grains from compacting too much.

Kiser's vegetable oil-coated sand treatment gives the same effect as wax and polymer, and it is also dust-free. It helps keep sand in place and add stability to it in a windy outdoor arena. It also doesn't need to be watered, and costs far less than wax or polymer. This blend is easy to apply and lasts for about two years before needing to be re-treated.

Attwood says a coated sand footing would be improved by adding fiber.

"If you add textiles to coated sand, you can make a really great footing that you don't have to water," he says. "So you're saving yourself water, you're saving yourself time maintaining it, and there's absolutely no dust. All the fine particles have been mopped up by the wax or polymer. So it keeps everything in your arena so clean."

Coated Sand Cons

A wax-coated sand surface is more expensive than pure sand blended with textiles, Attwood says. This is because of the additional ingredient and steps in the process.

Wax surfaces can be affected by extreme changes in temperature, such as hardening in cold weather and softening in hot weather. Wax can wear away from sand over time, requiring expensive re-waxing. It is also very sticky.

"The majority of these wax-coated sand and fiber footings have been developed in England," Attwood says. "I think those footings are really well-suited to the British climate, which never gets too hot, never gets too cold. It's a very temperate climate, and that's where they work their best. These footings are ubiquitous in Britain."

Note that you may have a hard time disposing of a wax surface at the end of its lifespan (see sidebar—p. 65).

A vegetable oil coating needs to be applied to very clean, pure sand, without silt or clay, otherwise it will be absorbed into the finer particles, Kiser says. This makes it unsuitable for most higher-intensity Western performance arenas, where the composition must include a mixture of sand and finer particles, and there's a risk of the base becoming too slick. Kiser also cautions against using a vegetable oil-coated sand on top of a limestone base. He has seen it make footing extremely hard, like concrete.

Grass

Although less common in arenas these days (as mentioned at the beginning of this chapter), grass is the footing choice for some competition arenas, such as certain jumping events and polo.

Attwood says, ultimately, in any footing they're

maintaining, arena footing managers are attempting to recreate the good qualities that a grass surface offers the horse.

The reason grass is preferable, he explains, is that grass allows for a small amount of sliding. This is because there are two layers to grass: the grass on the surface, which gives you the ability to slide slightly, and the underneath dirt, which is held together with roots—acting as a network of fibers.

"When footing is performing perfectly, if you take conventional sand blended with textiles, the bottom few inches are working as a kind of pad, and it's almost recreating grass. It's giving shock absorption," Attwood says. "You don't come to a stop in one jarring movement. That tends to be really good for legs, joints, and tendons."

Grass Pros
A grass arena is beautiful and traditional, and it offers both shock absorption and a bit of slide. Therefore, riding in a pasture is a workable option when you don't have an arena available, but it comes with its own set of challenges.

Grass Cons
Grass footing is difficult to maintain. Attwood says hoof traffic during an event will inevitably wear away the grass, even if it's immaculate at the start.

"I think if the grass is in great condition, it can be really good, but it only just lasts for the show," Attwood says. "You pretty much destroy it."

When a pasture gets too wet it can be dangerously

DISPOSING OF ARENA FOOTING

We don't often think about the end of the lifespan of arena footing, but disposal is an important consideration. Footing does not last forever, especially mixtures with wood particles. Outdoor arena footing tends to degrade faster than indoor footing.

"Equestrian Surfaces" says disposing of arena footing in a landfill should be a last resort, and it's an expensive option. A surface with wax or fiber may not be able to be used as a soil improver or agricultural top dressing. But sand and silt can be used to top-dress pastures and turnouts. Footing can be revitalized and used again, or used elsewhere on your property to address muddy arenas or high-traffic areas near gates, for example.

Every region and country has different rules about building arenas and disposing of footing. Make sure to research the options in your area to include in your considerations.

slippery or muddy from hooves tearing up the grass. When a pasture is too dry, the soil can crack and become perilous for your horse.

"It's fraught with danger," Attwood says. "There are also animals burrowing holes, and you don't want your horse to step in a hole."

Finding Surface Materials and Creating the Right Footing Blend

Attwood determines the gradation of sand by doing a *sieve analysis*, which is a series of sieves stacked on top of each other. The sample of material is placed in the top and shaken for about half an hour, until it works through about 12 sieves to the bottom. He then weighs each sieve and works out the percentage of material at each level.

"The top could be as big as marbles—half an inch—and the bottom is incredibly fine, often 200 microns," Attwood says. "Once you've done that, you get the relative percentage of all the sizes. This is massively important for both Western and English arenas."

The sieve analysis is also important when sourcing footing materials. For example, when purchasing sand, "Equestrian Surfaces" recommends first ordering a sieve analysis from the quarry or producer of the material to determine the ratio of sand, silt, and clay. Because clay dries into small balls that look like sand, skewing the results, sand is best screened wet.

"What you end up with is sand in your top screen, silt in the second screen, and your clay washes away," Kiser says. "You can't capture that."

After allowing the remaining material to dry completely, Kiser will weigh the sand and silt to figure out what percentage of the total weight of the sample he has left. The unknown weight is the clay that washed away. The clay percentage is determined by taking the sand and silt weight from the dry weight of the original sample.

Your source for footing material may vary. Kiser frequently changes his sources because a particular area can get mined out.

Austin says finding the right materials is the most difficult part of building or improving an arena.

"It is so hard getting the right material that is also easily transported to your arena site," Austin says. "People think it's easy to get; that it's on every corner. It is the toughest part of our job, without a doubt."

Austin often collaborates with Kiser on projects. He says he and Kiser may make a blend with materials from five different locations, test it, and when its within 80 percent of what they want, they'll transport

3.6 A–D A sieve analysis will determine the composition of your materials, helping you choose the right mix for your arena. The gradation of sand is determined by doing a wet sieve analysis, which is a series of sieves stacked on top of each other (A). Each sieve has holes of a different size, allowing sand of various diameters to pass through to the next level (B & C). After passing wet sand through each level to the last and finest sieve, what washes away—the unknown—is clay, the finest particle (D).

Footing | 67

3.7 Bob Kiser develops footing blends for arenas around the United States.

3.8 A & B Finding the right materials is the most difficult part of building an arena. Material can even vary from load to load, even originating from the same vendor or quarry. As you can see in A versus B, processing can also make a difference. A has larger chunks of material, while B is screened, with finer particles.

that blend to the arenas they are working on and fine-tune the mixture.

Be wary of quarries selling a blend of materials labeled as "arena footing," Austin says. "Nowhere is there footing for arenas that is pre-blended, ready to go, gets loaded into the dump truck, and delivered to your job site. That does not exist. It usually requires multiple blends in a region to be perfect. You might find the absolute perfect mix that doesn't require anything added to it, but that is like a needle in a haystack. It's pretty rare."

There are a number of companies that sell textiles you can incorporate into your arena footing. Attwood says three of the biggest are GGT, Premier Equestrian, and a German company called Bacher Equestrian Footing.

Randy Snodgress, owner of arena maintenance equipment company Arena Werks, says be careful of purchasing footing from a source unfamiliar with arenas. Without conscientious vetting, you could end up with truckloads of sand that has rocks or other trash in it.

"You need to go to the sand or gravel pit and get a sample of the material, and take it home to make sure it's the right composition, and see how it does when you add water and let it dry out," Snodgress warns. "Don't just take your neighbor's extra dirt and dump it in your arena."

THE BIGGEST EXPENSE

The biggest expense surrounding footing is the cost of transporting it from the mining location to your arena, says Kiser.

"Your product cost is fairly uniform, no matter where you go," he notes. "But your trucking is what's expensive."

Determining the Quality of Your Material

Natural Footing Materials

You just have to be there, says Kiser. As arena consultants, he and his son Jim make it a point to go on site at the origin location and play an active role in the selection. At the very least, you must be there when it's dumped at your arena location to make sure it meets your criteria.

"Don't just tell somebody to go to a pit and get it," Kiser says. "You have to check the materials."

Kiser uses a series of test tools to make sure the footing is correct. In addition to the sieve analysis (see p. 66), he does a compaction test with a hydraulic press. He also does a water retention test, and a sand, silt, clay analysis.

Manmade Footing Materials

For textiles, going with a reputable company is a good start, Attwood says. When purchasing carpet fiber, there are two main types of carpet. You can get trimmings from the edges of carpet rolls that are then chopped up, and Attwood says that is typically new, clean carpet material from the factory.

The other option is used carpet that has been shredded. This is usually cheaper, but the caveat is the foreign material that it could include. Typically this type of fiber comes from old carpet from homes, then rolled up and taken to be shredded. It can contain extraneous material such as paper clips, pencils, and hair clips, and Attwood says foreign items are not usually separated from the shredded carpet. He recommends avoiding fiber from these sources for this reason.

"Post-consumer waste, I think is a disaster [for arenas]," Attwood says. "You could end up with contaminants that could damage your horse's hooves. You also don't know what kind of carpet you're getting."

For arenas, you want a synthetic carpet that includes polyester, nylon, or polypropylene. Some used carpets include wool fibers, which Attwood says break down and cause problems for the footing.

3.9 Kiser uses many tools to test and blend footing mixtures for arenas!

"Make sure you ask what kind of carpet is in the shredded fibers," Attwood says. "And you need to avoid having natural fibers."

Footing Takeaway

Remember: To create the best footing, you not only need the right materials in the correct combination, but the moisture level must be adjusted continually and the arena surface needs proper dragging to promote a consistent loose depth on top of your arena base. You cannot have good footing, with even the best materials, without care and water.

CASE STUDY

BOB KISER'S STOCK HORSE ARENA FORMULA—
AND BEST PRACTICES FOR WESTERN EVENTS

When Bob Kiser began working with the arena footing for the National Reining Horse Association Futurity in Oklahoma City, Oklahoma, in the early 1990s, he experimented with a number of footing combinations. He settled on a mixture of about 73 percent sand, 15 percent silt, and the remainder being clay. Kiser knows this is the recipe because he's tested it with a wet sieve, which starts with a sample of sand that he screens into different gradations while washing the material, and once it is dry, weighing each level. The blend he came up with worked so well for the reining competition, the American Quarter Horse Association World Championship Show asked to use the same dirt at their event, held at the same facility.

"That dirt became the standard for every [stock horse breed] horse show facility in the country," Kiser says. "I don't know how many people took samples of that blend and tried to match it, even in other countries."

That blend has worked well for many different Western events, with the exception of barrel racing, which needs a slightly higher silt-clay content.

An arena mainly used for Western pleasure, Western all-around, or English flat classes is generally sandier than one prepared for Western performance horse events such as reining, cutting or cow horse. Kiser says this is to avoid compaction and to keep the footing consistent across the pen.

"If I was building an arena for trail classes, I'd make it sandier, but the top layer should be pretty shallow," Kiser says. "You don't want them to have to drag their feet out of the sand."

To make footing work for barrel racing requires expert management and maintenance, as the surface needs to be slightly heavier to handle the force the horse exerts as it hustles around the barrel. Kiser says a 68 percent sand, 16 percent silt, 16 percent clay blend is preferable for barrel racing.

Reining footing has closer to 75 percent sand.

3.10 Most Western arenas use a combination of three classes of soil: sand, silt and clay.

Kiser says reiners prefer a coarser gradation and more silt over clay, making it smoother for horses to perform sliding stops. Too much clay can make the ground too "grabby" for reiners, which is dangerous for stops where the horse needs to be able to melt into the ground and slide for a long distance.

"Reining is an event that defies the laws of physics, because you want a horse to be able to run down and stop 30 feet, but yet when he runs a fast circle, you don't want him to slip—and the horse has sliding plates on," Kiser says.

Cow horse events include a reining pattern and the horse and cow performing fast turns and hard stops, as well as a cutting class. For the reining and cow work, the ground should be close to reining footing, but include slightly more clay.

"You have to have ground that will hold these horses when they go down the fence," Kiser says. "But when you get a cow out in the middle of that arena and you're trying to stay up on his shoulder, and he's pushing on you, it gets a little scary. You need safe ground."

Footing for cutting requires more sand at one end where the cattle are worked. For reined cow horse events, which include both reining, working a single cow in the pen, and herd work the same format as cutting, it's a particular challenge.

"For the cutting [at a reined cow horse event], we have to bring some sand in, and then we have a very short amount of time—less than an hour—to scrape some of that and get it out of the arena, get the pens reset and get ready for the next event," Kiser says.

For barrel racing and rodeo, the footing ideally has a blend of sand with clay or sandy loam. Barrel racing ground crew manager Leland Smith says too much sand will be too loose for this event. He says competitors wants a deeper layer of sandy loam packed more firmly to avoid hitting the hard pan.

"We're looking for horses to be able to get in the dirt, but not slip or have it blow out from under their feet," Smith says.

Smith rips at least 8 inches into the footing, leaving a firmer base underneath. With added moisture and dragging, the footing should firm up to have six inches of top ground.

"That way the horses never hit that slick hard pan," Smith says. "We strive to pull the dirt back into the holes around the barrels, and if you're running 700 horses, we drag around the barrels every five—a big drag where we totally level the arena back out, rip up, lay it back down and start all over every 48 or 50. We're trying to make it solid for them to run on, but soft enough to run through."

CHAPTER 4
BUILDING AN ARENA

Building an arena involves more than ordering a load of sand and spreading it on a flat area of land. But the process doesn't have to be overwhelming. Follow a plan meticulously, and before you know it, you will be on your way to riding in a beautiful training space filled with footing just right for your horse.

This chapter outlines a couple of ways arena experts approach the process of constructing arenas. Their methods vary, as do the materials they use—but there are common principles to keep in mind regardless of where you live and the discipline you favor.

Beginning at the Bottom

To start, arenas typically have a distinct *base* and *top layer*, while some have a *middle layer* as well.

Arena Base

Regardless of the top layer's composition, a firm, stable, level base with excellent drainage is important (see sidebar, p. 76). The base needs to be durable enough to stand up to indirect impact from hooves, as well as maintenance equipment. It also helps maintain the proper moisture content. In areas that receive significant rainfall, installing a base with drainage is helpful. Base materials for these situations can include limestone or crushed gravel.

The base and the top layer should not mix. Too much moisture, incorrect maintenance, or riding when the top layer is saturated can cause mixing between the two levels.

A geotextile membrane—a fabric sheet designed to be used with soil—can be a helpful solution, according to "Equestrian Surfaces." This allows water to drain but does not allow sand to mix with the base. However, a geotextile membrane can become clogged with clay, reducing its ability to drain water. If the top layer is too shallow, the geotextile membrane can be torn, broken, and pulled up. Kiser uses a geotextile

4.1 A & B *Regardless of the top layer's composition, a firm, stable, level base with excellent drainage is important. The base needs to be durable enough to stand up to impact from hooves, as well as maintenance equipment. In an indoor natural footing arena, packed clay is often the base. (A). With the top layer in place (primarily consisting of 4 to 6 inches of sand, although it can and should be mixed with other ingredients), you would never guess how much care was given to prepare each layer underneath (B)!*

membrane only in an arena with an unstable sub-base (usually compacted soil beneath the base), or to keep rocks from migrating to the footing.

When you're building an outdoor arena, Kiser advises against installing a clay base with sand on top.

"Clay is an expansive soil," Kiser says. "Silt has less expansion, but sand doesn't expand or swell at all. When clay is packed together, there's almost no airspace between those particles. But when you introduce water, and water gets into it, the water will start to push some particles apart." This can result in mixing with your top layer. Sand doesn't percolate water back to the top of the footing very well. So if you get 2 inches of rain, very little runs off of pure

DRAINAGE

We have already touched on the fact that, no matter what kind of arena you have, it needs to be able to divert moisture away from it. How well your riding and training space handles water drainage is crucial to being able to use it, particularly when it is outdoors. But not every arena requires a complicated system of pipes. A well-made base can help with drainage.

New systems of drainage are constantly being developed. One recent evolution is the *Ebb and Flow* system—a method of adding moisture to your footing, or taking it away. This system is located underneath a top layer of sand, or sand and fiber, and water bubbles up from below to deliver consistent moisture across the arena with little evaporation. This system starts with a plastic liner placed 18 inches deep to contain the moisture. On top of the liner are pipes perforated with holes. Above the pipes is 8 inches of plain sand, and then 4 inches of footing on top of that. Near the arena is a round tank connected to a water source, which provides moisture when you need it. A valve system helps control whether you are boosting moisture (pumping water in), or subtracting it (pumping it out)—for example, in an outdoor arena after it rains.

Other common methods of arena drainage include digging a trench alongside one end of the arena, and connecting a network of pipes laid across the area under the footing surface.

Maintenance

When your arena has a deep drainage system, you'll need to plan for how you will clean any pipes that are involved, should they get clogged. You can place pipes in a design that makes it easy to clean later. Bob Kiser says this means including an area on an uphill side of the drainage lines where you can pump a high volume of water into the pipes to flush them out.

sand—it will go straight down to the clay and will eventually get absorbed by the clay. If the top looks dry, you may think it's rideable, but with a horse's or tractor's weight and impact of hooves, the wet clay base will separate and start pushing up through the sand.

"At that point, your arena is ruined," Kiser says.

Middle layer

Western sport arenas do not have a middle layer, Kiser says, but for English sports, a middle layer can offer additional stabilization and elasticity. Material for a middle layer can include shredded rubber or mats of elastic material such as polymer.

Top Layer

Regardless of discipline, the top layer should be stable, even, and consistent across the arena. "Equestrian Surfaces" says the top layer needs to "allow the hoof a certain amount of glide at touchdown, but still provide enough grip to maintain the confidence of the horse and rider." The top layer needs to absorb shock and also support the horse as he makes a turn.

The top layer primarily consists of sand, although as we covered in chapter 3, it can and should be mixed with other ingredients (see p. 56). Generally, the top layer should be 4 to 6 inches thick, depending on the desired use of the arena, and what the middle (if there is one) and base layers look like.

Construction Steps

There are many different ways to build an arena. In the pages ahead, I will discuss Nick Attwood's process for an outdoor arena primarily used for English riding (based on the type of footing used). I will also explain how Danny Austin and Bob Kiser construct outdoor, indoor, and covered arenas made with natural materials—sand, silt, clay—primarily used for Western disciplines. My goal in presenting the process each arena specialist uses is to point out important steps needed to creating a long-lasting, safe, and consistent riding and training space.

Outdoor Arena—English Disciplines: Step by Step

Note: the method of arena construction outlined in this section will start at around $8.00 a square foot, Attwood says. But the results are optimal.

> **EXPERT TIP**
>
> In general, Danny Austin says drainage systems do not work well with a hard base—such as the firmer lower layer that many reining and cow horse arenas require.

"You'll get an arena draining beautifully, fully contained, and working well," he says. "It's also going to last."

The timeframe from start to finish on a project like this one, a 100-by 200-foot arena, typically takes Attwood's crew around 10 days. That also depends on how far away materials are located.

Step 1: Choose a Location and Orientation
As mentioned in chapter 2, selecting the location of your arena is an important first step in the process. Attwood says you should consider the proximity to the barn, whether it's in a hilly area, what distractions are nearby, and where runoff water naturally flows. You'll also decide the orientation—which direction you have the long and short ends—at this time.

Step 2: Stake out the Perimeter
Attwood says generally the perimeter of the construction area should be at least 10 feet around the perimeter of the desired arena.

Step 3: Prepare the Pad
The arena is built atop a site resembling a pad where one would build a house, Attwood says. This starts by removing the topsoil, because topsoil does not offer stability, and it also contains organic material from grass.

"If you leave that topsoil under the arena, it will decompose and cause the arena to be unstable or potentially fall apart," explains Attwood.

He usually uses smaller equipment such as a skid steer (Bobcat®) to remove a 4- to 6-inch layer of ground in order to get to a firmer lower layer. This step usually takes a couple of days, depending on how much dirt has to be moved.

Step 4: Grade the Slope
Next, the pad site is graded into a gentle slope. Attwood does *not* recommend a crown—where two slopes come to a peak in the center of the arena. When your arena is likely to receive significant rainfall, he prefers sloping it in one direction to about 1 to 1.5 percent grade difference.

"What that means is, if it's a 1.5 percent slope, if the width is 100 feet, it's going to be 18 inches lower at one end than the other," Attwood says. "I think more than 1.5 percent you will definitely notice when you're riding that you're riding uphill or downhill. So 1.5 percent is a good compromise."

Step 5: Compact the Pad
The pad needs to be solid, Attwood notes. When it's not, you'll need to compact it with a roller. When your area's native soil is a high percentage of sand, it'll

drain extremely well, but it may not be stable enough to build an arena without some modifications.

"If it's not the right material, it may never compact," Attwood says. "Then you'll probably need to get some kind of fill dirt, or a material with a lot of stability to it."

In a location such as South Carolina, Attwood has added anywhere from 12 to 18 inches of an alternative material such as fill dirt to a pad site, then graded it and rolled it until it's firm and tight—a good pad on which to build an arena.

"It needs to be good and tight and solid before you do the next layer," Attwood says. "It needs to be graded, rolled, and compacted to be as straight and true as possible."

Step 6: Dig a Trench

On the lower side of the arena, Attwood digs a trench, using a backhoe. It's usually around 18 inches deep. This is where excess water from the arena will drain through.

Step 7: Build Containment

Once the pad is prepared, you'll want to add a method of containment, so your arena footing doesn't blow away or get washed away when it rains. Attwood's team will sink 4-inch by 4-inch posts, every 4 feet around the arena. If the arena will have a fence, the posts will extend 5 feet out of the ground. If there will be a shorter fence, or no fence, Attwood will put shorter posts in the ground—at least 12 inches above the pad.

On the inside of these posts, he'll lay pressure-treated boards, which are then screwed to the posts on the inside, creating a perimeter. This makes a wall that is 12 inches tall. Attwood uses wood that is high-quality ground contact lumber designed to resist rotting when in the ground or when it gets wet.

"Now we've created what looks like an empty sandbox or a swimming pool," Attwood says.

Do not neglect containment around the entrance to the arena, he adds. Without containment, the footing will migrate out of the arena, resulting in a low spot in that area. This is true for an outdoor arena, and *especially* for an indoor arena.

"Without containing the entrance, you're going to introduce inconsistencies and maintenance problems down the road," Attwood says. "The footing is going to get thinner and thinner in that area, and eventually somebody is going to get into the base with the drag."

The steps from grading to compacting to building the containment can take a few days.

Step 8: Add a Layer of Fabric
Next, Attwood will cover the prepared dirt with a woven polypropylene fabric.

"This material is commonly found in road construction," Attwood says. "It's relatively inexpensive."

Step 9: Lay Perforated Pipe
On top of the woven fabric, Attwood will lay perforated pipe across the arena that will be covered by arena footing, except for the ends. This will help drain water away from the arena surface.

Step 10: Top with Drain Rock
Attwood places a 4- or 5-inch layer of drain rock on top of the pipe(s), fabric, and trench. He will grade this layer to be as true and level as possible.

Step 11: Lay Down More Fabric
This layer of fabric is completely different than the woven material in Step 8. Attwood says it is non-woven and resembles felt. It's used for filtration and to separate layers.

"The felt that we use is pretty thick—I'd say it's almost ¼-inch thick, and it's pretty heavy," he says.

This fabric needs to be perfectly smooth and flat atop the drain rock with no wrinkles or creases. To achieve this, Attwood uses rolls of felt, and rolls one or two pieces out at a time, overlapping each piece by about 18 inches, gluing them together, and then adding to those sections before going to the next rolls. Attwood suggests overlapping in a way that mimics shingles on a roof, taking care that water can't get into the overlapped areas.

"We will do this piecemeal," Attwood says. "Constantly keeping it taut and tight as we go along, constantly making sure there aren't any ripples or folds in the fabric. You don't want to lay all the fabric out in one go, and then come back the next day and it has blown away."

This step can take one to two days to complete.

Step 12: Add the Footing
In the prepared area, the next step is to add 4 or 5 inches of properly mixed footing on top of the fabric material. With 4 or 5 inches of drain rock, then 4 or 5 inches of footing, you should still have 1½ inches of the containment boards showing all the way around the arena.

Mixing the footing prior to laying it in the arena can take a couple of days.

"In a 100- by 200-foot classic outdoor arena—20,000 square feet—we would use around 500 tons of drain rock and about 350 tons of footing for the top." Attwood says.

BUILDING ON A BUDGET

If the cost of the premium construction process is outside your budget for an outdoor arena, Attwood says, at minimum, you must excavate the topsoil and put it in a pile to the side while preparing the pad, to avoid organic material compromising your base layer.

"I've seen people skip that step, and it often doesn't end well," he warns.

You also need to grade the pad to be as straight and true as possible. Attwood says a slope is preferable, but it needs to be a flat plane (like a tilted board, not an ocean floor). He explains the latter will lead to inconsistencies in the layers placed on top of the pad.

You'll still need to have a method of containment. Attwood says some facilities use railroad ties.

Next, you can add a 4- to 6-inch layer of stone dust, also called "quarter minus limestone or decomposed granite." Particles are anywhere from ¼ of an inch to dust in size.

"Some places call it 'screenings,' some places call it 'stone dust'—it has a lot of different names around the country," Attwood says. "But the most important thing is, you don't want particles bigger than ¼ of an inch. Otherwise, you'll end up with stones."

Stone dust is made by crushing rock, and the gravel is then passed through a screen with gaps of a ¼-inch. The dust that falls through is what is used. You want to avoid material with larger stones (such as rocks 1 to 1½ inches in size) because when these rocks eventually rise to the surface due to their large size, they'll leave a hole in the base, and footing will fall into the hole.

"Eventually the base in that area is going to start to fall apart," Attwood says. "Once it falls apart, you're going to have rocks in your footing, and you'll be riding on rocks, which can cause your horse to get a stone bruise."

If you have a smaller particle size, even if the horse digs into the material and knocks a few ¼-inch or smaller stones out of that layer, the foundation is less likely to fall apart.

After laying the stone dust, you'll want to roll it, compact it, and add water to get it very stable. Attwood says some riders will leave about 1 inch of it looser on top and actually ride on this surface. It's not ideal, though—Attwood notes when it dries out, it's very dusty, and if it rains and dries, it can become a very hard surface.

"It's not impossible, but it can be quite difficult to maintain and drag to keep a fluffy surface on it, a looser surface, because that material is designed to compact down and give a solid foundation," Attwood says.

(continued)

Mid-Budget Option

If you have a little more in the budget, you can start with the stone dust configuration, and then add about a 1-inch layer of sand on top. Then, drag with the teeth down to blend the top layer of stone dust with the sand to make a slightly less compact top layer.

"It gives you a little bit more give, a little bit more life to the footing," Attwood says.

The disadvantages are similar, though. It's still going to get very dusty, and it's still going to get hard after it rains. But on the upside, this structure tends to hold up, even with heavy rainfall.

Another option is to add textiles. Both of these added materials will give the footing more bounce and a fluffier texture (see chapter 3, p. 56, for more about this option). The downside to using these materials on a stone dust base is when it rains, the water will pool and take longer to dry via evaporation instead of draining away.

Building an arena is an expensive endeavor, but use caution with where you cut costs if budget is a concern, Attwood says. This includes the footing itself.

"We want to use the right amount of footing, we want to add the right amount of textiles to the footing, and we want to use the highest quality textiles that we can get," Attwood says.

EXPERT TIP

Small cleats on your tractor tires are helpful to preserve entrances and exits to your arena. "You want to make it easy for the tractor to get in and out," Attwood says.

Step 13: Reinforce the Containment

In areas where a tractor goes in and out of the arena, it is good to reinforce the entranceway with a threshold to keep the footing in place.

Step 14: Replace the Topsoil

You will now place the topsoil you removed at the beginning of the process around the outer perimeter of the containment boards, leaving about 2 inches of the board visible at the top.

Outdoor Arena—Western Disciplines: Step by Step

The planning and install of an outdoor arena for Western disciplines can take up to six months, but the actual building is usually only 10 to 30 days, Austin says.

Step 1: Earthwork

Once you are done planning, including how the arena is going to be positioned at the site, you'll start the earthwork.

"We locate all of our preliminary four corners of the actual arena, then figure out how much area we

4.2 In preparation for your arena site, remove several inches of the topsoil using a skid steer.

have to disturb to get all of our drainage and flow lines," Austin says.

This includes sloping the area *away* from the arena a minimum of 5 to 6 feet all around the perimeter, to allow rainwater to flow around the arena, not through it. This is a *buffer zone.*

Then you will remove the topsoil and rootzone, stockpiling for future use in landscaping and backfill around the perimeter.

Step 2: Hydrate and Scarify

Austin will take an implement with ripper teeth to the entire surface, and will then hydrate the area with water.

"Just like baking a cake, you can't bake a dry cake," he says. "So we get everything ripped and blended, and then we bring our moisture up to what we call 'optimum for compaction.'"

Step 3: Grading and Sloping

Austin says his outdoor pens do not have more than a 1 percent slope—he aims for 0.7 to 1 percent, and drains across the width.

"We don't drain them on the diagonal, just the short side," Austin says. "So on a 100- by 200-foot arena, the length is completely level, and it only slopes 0.7 percent to 1 percent along the width."

Next is grading and adding fill dirt. The base is made of limestone outdoors. Austin says he does not put more than a 6-inch layer of fill at a time. Once the fill dirt has been added, he goes over the layer with a compacting machine until it is flat and ready for the next layer.

"We don't go out and put 2 or 3 feet of fill down," Austin says. "It's done in multiple compacted layers so the arena doesn't settle."

Austin laser-grades the pad to make sure it's exactly flat and at the right slope. Your grading must be a priority—do not try to save money on this step, he says.

"You can't cut corners on the grading," he warns. "It's got to be done correctly, no matter what surface we put on it."

If your budget means you cannot complete your arena all at once, and you choose to do the grading step and footing later, Austin says you should aim to keep the pad site as free of vegetation as possible.

Step 4: Fencing

Depending on your fence type, some fence posts need to be installed as soon as the actual pad work is done, Austin says.

"Other fences are put in after we do our base layer. So if they'll be 'drill posts' versus 'drive posts'—we

4.3 *In order to solidify your base layer, use a roller to compact it as you build.*

EXPERT TIP

Austin and Kiser often work together on projects. Kiser says drainage for an arena built for Western disciplines is challenging, because you need to contain the footing—keep the sand and silt from eroding out of the arena—which can hamper drainage. One solution they've found is to dig a trench, line the trench with a piece of non-woven fabric, then lay a drainpipe into the trench. Next, fill the trench with pea gravel covering the drainpipe. Then lay another piece of fabric over the top and fasten it to a railroad tie to secure it. You then build your arena fence on the inside of the railroad tie.

"It's not a perfect method, but if you don't use this system, you'll have sand wash under that [railroad tie]," Kiser says. "Eventually, it'll fill up your drainage line. But the reason you run your fabric over the top of the railroad tie is so that it'll bring the ties together tightly and sand won't get through as easily."

Kiser does not add a layer of fabric under the entire arena, unless the underlying surface is unstable, or there's a risk of the rock traveling up into the footing. He does because of drag concerns.

"What will happen is you're going to get somebody that goes into the arena to drag, and it's gotten out of level, and they let their rippers down too far," Kiser says "Then you'll start seeing pieces of fabric coming up out of the footing."

---

meet with the fence contractor and decide what's the appropriate measure."

The fencing contractor will install the fence, usually before the footing is put down, Austin says. This reduces damage to the arena footing.

"Worst case scenario, if we go and do a finished surface, and then it is fenced, they could destroy all of the footing at the perimeter," Austin says. "So we may put in the base, let them build the fence or they build the fence before we do the base, but either way, we never put the [top level] footing down before the fence is built."

Step 5: Installing the Footing
Once the base is ready and the fence is built, Austin will install the footing, unless there's an irrigation system that needs to go in first.

"On an outdoor, we prefer a [tractor-pulled] water trailer arrangement over any kind of irrigation," Austin and Kiser say.

Covered or Indoor Arena: Step by Step
A covered or an indoor arena can take a while to erect—Austin has worked on one that took a year to complete, from the time they broke ground, due to permit snags and supply chain issues. But if everything is lined up, schedules coincide, and there are

no permits needed, an arena—including putting up the building—can be done in about six months. The actual structure construction can be done in less than 30 days.

Step 1: Select Location and Grade

As with an outdoor, select your site and prepare by removing top soil, adding fill dirt, and grading. But Austin says you don't need to laser grade at this point—that step comes later.

Step 2: Build the Structure

After planning your site, then finding a building company for the structure and grading the pad, you can expect to build the cover or structure as the next step.

"We get all the grading done, then I'll meet with the building contractor, and the concrete contractor, if that isn't done in-house, and go over all the details with them," Austin says. "We discuss where the drainage patterns are, we caution tape off the graded area, and make sure they understand where the corners of the arena are."

For a covered arena, next typically comes the concrete foundation, which involves drilling.

"That's when the pad gets destroyed, because the heavy equipment is running over it trying to get the building up before it rains sometimes," Austin says.

This is why Austin anticipates going back over the pad to make it perfect (the reason you didn't laser grade in earlier steps), because he knows it'll most likely get disrupted and will need to be repaired.

The equipment used to build a cover or indoor structure is very heavy and can destroy a pad or base in seconds, Austin says. *Do not* build the arena surface before the roof and/or sides. You want your footing to be your final step.

Step 3: Remove Debris and Grade Again

After the building or cover has been installed, Austin will go over the pad site with a drag with a small ripper and magnetic comb to pick up as much construction debris as possible.

"Unfortunately, a lot of times, screws and nails get dropped by crews from the building company or concrete company," Austin says. "We will pick up all the debris we can, then switch back to a grading mode to hydrate the surface, bring it back to life, and then put the perfect laser finish on it."

EXPERT TIP

In a Western indoor or covered arena, you're looking for moisture to drain off as soon as possible—rain can come in the sides when only covered. But most arenas do not have a drainage system underneath unless there's groundwater.

"In a sand, silt, and clay arena, water will kill it," Danny Austin says. "Water turns dirt to mud."

Step 4: Install Fencing and Amenities

Similar to the outdoor arena, the next step is fencing or kickwalls. Also lighting, fans, mirrors, and any other structural amenities to finish out all the features on the covered or indoor arena.

"They can all work pretty much at the same time, as well as your electrician for your lights and your fans—they don't disrupt each other," Austin says.

Step 5: Add Footing

After all of the other elements have been added, Austin will go back to do a final trim of the base and make sure there are no contaminants (foreign material). He will then bring in and install the footing.

A

> **EXPERT TIP**
>
> An indoor base in an arena for English disciplines usually consists of a minimum of 4 inches of stone dust or similar material, compacted to 95 percent with moisture. It is then rolled with a 0 percent grade, unlike an outdoor base, that is sloped.
>
> Covered and indoor arenas for Western sports have a clay base.

"There are a lot more steps for an indoor arena," Austin says. "I take another role, rather than just that of a footing specialist. At that point I make sure the whole site stays together throughout each step, because usually each company is working on its own project and they don't realize the whole building is really just going up to protect the rectangle they're working on. A lot of people think the project is about the building, but the main reason you're building a structure is to protect the footing."

4.4 A–C *Regardless of the top layer's composition, a firm, stable, level base with excellent drainage is important. Base layer material in an indoor arena built for Western disciplines is made of clay, as seen here, added in 6-inch layers, then compacted until it is flat and ready for the next layer.*

Building an Arena

Building Your Building Team

Who is involved in building an arena? Here are some recommendations for building your own "building team" from our experts:

- Arena specialist—"Some of the best money you will spend will be for an arena specialist as a consultant," Kiser says.

- A general contractor to manage the entire project.

- Someone proficient in operating smaller construction equipment for grading and compacting the ground. Experience with arenas is a plus, but the equipment operator should at least be proficient with building site or road work.

- Subcontractors for drainage, structures, fencing, electrical, irrigation, fans, lights, and any other amenities (unless you have a general contractor taking care of everything).

Where do you find the professionals to build an arena? You can start with searching for arena building companies in your area. You can also ask arena footing companies for recommendations. If you're using textiles in your footing, for example, you might be able to get names of building professionals that work with your chosen footing company. Arena consultants can guide you to qualified contractors.

Word-of-mouth is your best method, Attwood says. Ask the owners of good equestrian facilities for recommendations. Your local footing company, soil company, civil engineers, or custom home builders might be able to help you find someone, Austin says. You can also find out who built arenas that you are familiar with that you know *aren't* optimal, so you can avoid those contractors.

Austin says your arena specialist or footing vendor needs to work together with the subcontractors you may hire, such as a fencing company, or if you're working on an indoor facility, the building and concrete companies.

"Your arena guy has to understand he needs to be on board throughout the process or there's going to be major problems—something is going to happen," Austin says. As mentioned in the earlier recommended building steps, "When an arena company completely builds your surface, and the building company follows with a structure, they will drill holes and get contaminants everywhere."

Austin says many good arena builders are inundated with work these days. When he is too booked to take on a project, he says he and Kiser tend to look to refer potential clients to other individuals knowledgeable in earthwork with the right laser-grounded equipment to start the process. These can include a parking lot builder, a house pad builder, or even a golf course builder.

"We try to find somebody who knows the mechanics of proper grading, and has the skillset that can do quality earthwork, and then we can guide him with the rest of it," Austin says.

He does not recommend hiring a landscape maintenance company—he has personally taken on many projects to repair arenas built by these kinds of companies. He also says steer clear of someone who seems overly focused on marketing at the possible expense of doing solid work.

"The guy you want is not one with flashy wraps on his truck or posting on Facebook every 10 minutes," Austin says. "The guys that are under the radar are the ones you want to look for. Someone who has a good reputation in a community."

Ultimately, building an arena is about finding and installing the right materials. This can be a challenge, depending on your location.

"For one job, I drove over 2,000 miles in a week in a 100-mile radius, searching every pit for materials, and then we ended up making a blend out of three different materials," Austin says. "Material selection is critical. You can't just call up Home Depot and say, 'Hey, I need arena base and I need arena sand.' It doesn't exist. There are no standards or rules on materials."

What to Ask Prospective Contractors

Experience—Find out how much experience a builder has in constructing arenas specifically, and even better, if they've built arenas for your chosen discipline. When in doubt, you can ask a credible arena specialist, who may not have availability to handle your project, to at least help you vet a potential contractor.

References—Ask for references from consultants, contractors, and subcontractors. Attwood says the more good arenas someone has helped build, the better your chances of ending up with a good arena yourself. He recommends going and visiting arenas they've had a part in completing when possible.

More Than Photos—Don't work with someone who sends you photos but will not give you references of facilities where you can tour their finished product.

Older Examples—Ask to see arenas they have worked on that are older than six months and have withstood weather and climate stressors, such as rainstorms.

Process—Ask the builder or contractor or specialist what their process looks like. Ask them to describe their methods. Attwood stresses the way he builds arenas is not the only correct method. Austin says that while you may not be able to tell how knowledgeable a builder is from asking him to summarize his process, when he doesn't mention a certain method of grading correctly, it's a red flag.

Payment—It's always wise to discuss the method and timeline of payment(s) for your contractors and builders. This way you know how much you'll need to pay upfront, throughout the process, and upon completion.

Your Responsibility

The advice given here on building an arena is sound, but our experts recommend consulting a professional before beginning the process of building your own arena to avoid making costly or time-consuming mistakes. Every arena, location, footing, and maintenance situation is different, so you want to be sure you have the right setup for your unique space.

"You should really get some professional help to make sure you are using the right materials and a solid plan," Attwood says.

Attwood says building an arena is not necessarily difficult to do, but the attention to detail at every step is important to make sure it's done well before moving on.

"Each individual layer needs to be completed correctly," Attwood says. "Every single step needs to be done to a certain standard, otherwise it may look fine and may work fine for a couple of weeks or months, but eventually it's going to fall apart, and it'll be a struggle to fix everything."

This may sound overly cautious, but Attwood emphasizes that building a safe arena is our responsibilities as the caretakers of horses.

"We are asking horses to do things they wouldn't do on their own, so it's our responsibility to provide them with a surface that is as safe as possible," Attwood says. "By definition, when the footing is safe, it's almost certainly going to be good. The footing is going to have the right properties, it's not going to be too hard or too deep, and it's as consistent as possible. That is the objective. That is your responsibility."

CHAPTER 5
MOISTURE MANAGEMENT

The greatest influence on your arena's performance will be moisture level. The ideal amount for a particular arena surface depends on many factors, including the type of arena footing and the chosen discipline.

"The amount of moisture that you have on a surface has a profound effect," Nick Attwood says. "You can have too little, and you can have too much moisture. Getting the right amount of moisture is critical to the way the footing performs."

The Right Amount of Moisture

Attwood explains that adding moisture to an arena with sand—or sand with textiles—binds the sand together, which enhances its riding suitability. The properties of *firmness, grippiness,* and *responsiveness* are all tied to the amount of moisture in the surface. So the relationship to moisture is key.

Moisture management is the most critical part of arena maintenance, Bob Kiser says. "When you've got the right knowledge on moisture management and on how to drag an arena, you can take a pretty mediocre arena and make it pretty nice, but I could build you the best arena anybody has ever had, and if you don't know how to control the moisture, how deep to drag, what to use to drag it with, you're going to ruin a really nice arena," he notes. "The way you drag an arena and the way you control your arena moisture is almost as important as the material you use."

With the right amount of moisture, you get:

Consistency—When you are using a natural footing material without any polymers, waxes, or oils, you must add water to get the right consistency for horses.

Rebound—This is the footing characteristic that provides a "springy" feeling to horse and rider. "Water puts a bit of a void between particles," Kiser says.

5.1 Moisture management is the most critical part of arena care. When you use a natural footing without any polymers, waxes, or oils, you must add water to achieve the correct consistency.

"That's where you get your cushion. And with a natural material, you don't have much rebound. It's a fairly flat material, unlike footing with synthetics that offers more rebound."

Stability—As footing dries out, it becomes less stable and will more easily push away from the horse's foot. You'll have less "purchase," Kiser says. Adding water adds weight and resistance.

Longevity—If you have textiles such as felt and fiber added to your footing, keeping the footing at the correct moisture content may prolong the life of that material, says Attwood. "It's going to keep the textiles mixed in with the footing so it won't blow or wash away. It will help keep the formula consistent and prevent the textiles from coming to the surface."

Too Little Moisture

"Completely dry, plain sand is not going to have enough support," Attwood says. "It's going to be deep, it's not going to be grippy enough, it's going to have too much slide, and it's not going to have any bounce to it. It's going to be completely 'dead.' So you want to improve all of those properties to make it safer for the horse. You want to get the right firmness; you want the right amount of grippiness, and the right amount of rebound. Those properties are key to maintaining the health of your horse. Without water, it's going to be incredibly difficult to do that."

Moisture also controls the dust in the arena. Randy Snodgress says a dusty arena will negatively affect the health and performance of the horses and riders using the pen day after day. Studies show that too much dust in an arena can contribute to inflammatory respiratory diseases, and when a horse inhales too much dust, it can increase mucus in the trachea, reducing the availability of oxygen, and consequently, negatively impact a horse's performance.

Too Much Moisture

Sand without moisture is difficult for riding, but if you keep adding moisture—or your arena experiences heavy rainfall—you will have too much of a good thing, and instead of holding the sand together, that water will create a soupy texture, Attwood says.

Saturated footing can be dangerous for your horse—it can lead to overextension of legs and injuries, Sydney Cannon says. Cannon is a graduate student at the University of Kentucky, studying biosystems and agricultural engineering. She is researching the use of water trucks at racetracks.

One way to tell if your footing is too wet is by the way your horse moves across it. Attwood says if your horse slips or struggles with getting a grip on the footing, it's far too wet to be ridden on. When there is any standing water, Cannon says avoid riding on that surface.

When you have an outdoor arena, handling weather like heavy rain will be a concern. For a pen with a clay hard base and a sand/silt mixture on top, Kiser recommends smoothing off the top layer to seal it from excess water, making it easier to shed that water instead of it filtering down to the base.

"Every one of those footprints holds a coffee cup of water," Kiser says. "That soaks in. So drag your arena and get it smoothed off before it rains. Get it compacted as much as you can."

For the arenas he builds, Kiser doesn't normally install underground drainage systems (see p. 76), preferring instead to perfect the mix of material. Austin does not install drainage systems for outdoor arenas either.

It's unusual for an indoor arena to receive enough water to flood, but open sides or windows, improper watering methods, or even changing the discipline that's using the arena can mean unsuitable levels of moisture.

Indoor or outdoor, if your arena with natural material is too wet, Kiser says all you can do is wait for it to get drier. You must look past the very top layer of your footing to check moisture before riding or dragging.

"You want to dig down and see how wet the lower layer is," he explains. "If you can take a handful of footing, squeeze it, and it squishes out of your fingers, you need to stay off it for at least another day. It's too wet. If it's a little soft, but doesn't try to mash out of your hand, then you're all right."

When you have wet soil, Kiser says the water leaves in two ways: it either goes down or it comes up. "The warmer it is outside, the more water percolates back to the top and evaporates," he explains. "Think about when you look across a field with the soil worked up on a warm day. You'll see the water coming up—it's like a mirage effect that you see on deserts."

You want to give your wet footing time for the moisture to percolate back to the top. If you break up the surface by dragging it, for example, you've loosened the top, and air has been worked into the layer, so that slows down the percolating process, leaving the lower layers to dry more slowly.

Kiser says moisture doesn't percolate up through sand as well as it does clay, due to the particles being farther apart in sand. "A lot of what I've learned about footing was learned through farming for 50 years—seeing how soil worked and how it dried, and how to get it dry. I learned pretty early on that if you have a wet place in a field, leave it alone and it will dry three times faster than if you 'mud it up.'"

Depending on how it was constructed, riding on a too-wet arena can destroy your base and ruin your arena.

"If the base is wet and you ride on your arena, punching into the base with your horse's hooves, at some point someone will have to come back and redo the base," Snodgress says. "But there's a safety factor too. If the ground is too sticky from being too wet, and your horse turns quickly without the right amount of give…or if it's even more wet and it's slick, your horse can slip and fall, risking injury to horse and rider."

Consistency

Just as important as the amount of moisture added to your footing is *consistency*: that moisture needs to be in the same amounts across the arena.

"There are scientists that believe that inconsistencies in footing can be just as detrimental to the health of the horse as having it too firm or too loose,"

EXPERT TIP

It's a myth that dragging will make your arena dry out faster. If the top layer is a little dry but the bottom is still wet, Kiser says dragging will actually disrupt the drying-out process. "It'll look like it's dried out faster because you dragged it and the top 'grays off' and it looks like it's drying, but if you dig down, it'll still be mud underneath."

Attwood says. "It's very important to have a consistent watering system."

Attwood says ideally, if you have 4 inches of sand/felt/fiber footing, the bottom 3 inches should contain more water, because that binds the footing together. The top inch, however, can be a little bit drier.

"When the footing works at its best, you have 3 inches knitted together with fiber and felt and water, forming a perfect pad that isn't hard, but a horse won't dig into it," Attwood says. "On top of that, you have a little bit of footing—half an inch or an inch that's a bit drier, allowing the horse to move and slide, which makes it comfortable for the horse because they have the right amount of grip."

Methods of Adding Moisture

There are a variety of ways you can manage the water content of your arena footing, and what's best will depend on your location, arena type, and budget.

Above-Ground

Rainwater
Relying on Mother Nature to keep your outdoor arena at the proper moisture level is unlikely to give you consistent results from day to day.

"It's not reliable—you don't get a quarter inch of rain every night, which would be perfect," Attwood says. "The good thing about outdoor rain showers, is when it does rain, it's a very consistent way of watering because the whole arena is getting about the same amount of moisture. But relying on the rain—that is not going to work as a management method."

Collecting rainwater and applying it using a water truck or trailer may be a better option to capitalize on storms—but you still may need to supplement from your water supply.

Hand-Watering
This is an inefficient and ineffective method of watering your arena, say our experts. A single sprinkler attached to a hose is also not a good solution because of the time required to cover the entire space (moving the sprinkler at intervals) and the inability to evenly apply water to your surface.

"You can't tell how wet you're getting the arena, how many gallons you're putting on an area," Kiser says. "[Hand-watering] is by far the worst method."

EXPERT TIP

Depending on rainwater for moisture often results in getting too much rain at one time for an arena build for Western disciplines and events, Kiser says. You actually want to protect your outdoor Western arena from rainwater by sealing it off before a storm.

MOISTURE METHODS PROS V. CONS

METHOD	PROS	CONS
RAINWATER	• Free • Consistent across surface	• Wildly unreliable as sole source of moisture
HAND-WATERING	• Inexpensive • Low-tech • Only ideal for small round pens	• Inefficient • Ineffective • The most time-consuming method • Not consistent across surface
SPRINKLER SYSTEM	• Convenient • Can be run without supervision at off times	• Often not thorough or consistent • Expensive for larger arenas • Gets surrounding surfaces and structures wet • Can drip onto surface, which can affect integrity of footing • Unusable in below-freezing temperatures • Excess water evaporation due to wind or hot weather can reduce amount of water reaching the surface
WATER TRUCK	• Largest tank capacity • Distributes water the fastest • Ideal for arid climates	• Expensive • Difficult to apply a consistent amount across footing • Can add too much moisture • Can damage footing due to excess weight of truck • Requires skilled driver

METHOD	PROS	CONS
WATER TRAILER	• Easy, even distribution of water • Best control of water flow and volume • Some models can water quickly	• Cost of trailer and tractor • Requires skilled driver
EBB AND FLOW	• Consistent moisture across arena with little evaporation • Precise control • Can help dry arena after rain • Acts as drainage when installed outdoors.	• Expensive • Arena must be absolutely flat to work • Does not work with silt or clay soils • Requires a specialist to install
ARENAWET™	• Consistent moisture across arena with little evaporation • Controlled by zones with precise release of water amounts • Can help dry arena after rain • Excellent feel for horses • Can be installed on a slope • Does not allow for bacteria growth	• Expensive • Does not work with silt or clay soils • Requires a specialist to install
HIT ACTIVE-AQUA	• Substantial savings on water usage • Precise control of moisture application	• Expensive • Does not work with silt or clay soils • Requires a specialist to install

The only space where hand-watering might make sense is if you're watering a round pen in the summer, Attwood says.

"[Hand-watering] is very time-consuming, and not a great way of watering," Attwood says.

Sprinkler System

There are several kinds of sprinkler systems available. You can install sprinkler heads around the perimeter of an outdoor arena, positioned so the water shoots up to 180 degrees from each head. Attwood says some horse facilities will have six to eight sprinkler heads, depending on the size of the arena.

"Those sprinkler heads generally run one at a time—that's the simplest way to make them work," Attwood says. "They're controlled by a timer, each one runs for about five minutes, and then the next sprinkler will go off, and it goes around the arena until each one is done."

The greatest benefit to this system is convenience, Attwood says. You can water your arena without supervision, setting a timer to have it run at an ideal time.

The disadvantage often found with these kinds of systems is the sprinklers don't do a thorough or consistent job of watering the arena. The sprinkler heads tend to spray in a circular pattern, which makes even application of water difficult.

"There will be places where the water patterns overlap; there will be places where it doesn't overlap," Attwood says. "There are places where if the wind is blowing strongly from one direction in an outdoor arena, some spots will never see any moisture."

If your arena is over 100 feet wide, you'll need more powerful sprinkler heads to cover the space, which are much more expensive than regular sprinkler heads. You will also need a powerful pump and large amounts of water available at one time to spray water from 40 or 50 feet away from the perimeter of the arena.

In indoor arenas, the most common system is overhead sprinklers installed in rows across the ceiling. This results in more of a "misting mechanism," where light amounts of water fall down to the surface.

"For an indoor, you have a much better chance of getting a more even distribution of moisture with overhead sprinkler heads," Attwood says.

The disadvantage here is it tends to get everything wet. When you have an indoor arena housed in a wooden building, or if it has wooden kickwalls, Attwood says the water spraying can deteriorate the material, and it can lead to mold and other issues.

Sprinkler systems also tend to drip—particularly annoying when they're overhead. And Attwood says they are not a good method for below-freezing winter temperatures.

"Those systems need to be flushed out in the winter," Attwood says. "You can't really have a sprinkler system full of water when it freezes. You're going to get burst pipes. So they tend to not work in the winter once it drops below freezing."

Kiser prefers not to use sprinkler systems, especially outdoors, because they don't water in a consistent pattern.

The only type he's seen that works is in the mold of "traveling gun irrigation"—where the sprinkler moves along a track—but the heads have to be the right size to be effective.

"The really good ones are big ones, but they shoot out a big stream of water, and if it's very windy, you'll lose quite a bit of water that way," Kiser says.

He does note that indoors, some overhead traveling systems can work well. They typically consist of a long bar across the ceiling with sprinkler heads that move at intervals across the arena.

"They do an excellent job on an indoor arena," Kiser says. "But they're almost unheard of in the United States. They're more common in Europe."

Water Truck

A water truck is another method to add moisture to your arena. It's a dedicated vehicle with a tank of water on the back end, outfitted to spray water out the back and to the sides. Such trucks are a hefty investment at over $50,000 at the time of writing, well outside the price range of most home arenas. They can, however, be extremely useful for competition arenas.

Attwood says the advantage of a water truck is how much water it can hold—1,500 to 2,000 gallons of water at a time. It sprays out quickly and can take just 10 minutes to empty.

OPTIONS FOR DRY CLIMATES

When your barn or facility has a limited water supply, you must consider how to add moisture and what kind of costs that process might add. Options may include:

- Buy water and store in a tank on the premises.
- Collect rainwater, during wet seasons to use during dry seasons.
- Install a *waxed sand surface*, which needs much less added moisture.
- Install a subsurface watering system, such as ArenaWet™ which uses less water and reduces evaporation.

"This can be important in a horse show situation where you're only given five minutes to water and drag in between classes," Attwood says.

But it is difficult to apply water consistently from a water truck, he admits. This is particularly true for jumping arenas.

"You find yourself going on the same track all the time, and you end up putting more water in certain spots," Attwood says. "We find when we're managing arena footing for a show, and we're using water trucks, there'll be a couple of places in the arena getting more water than anywhere else. You do have to manage that and try to stop the spray of water when you go through those parts to keep it as consistent as possible."

Kiser does not recommend water trucks, for several reasons.

"Water trucks are for construction sites," Kiser says. "They put out too much volume of water, and you've got this big truck driving around out there, and you can't really tell what you're doing. They can also displace footing when they turn."

Water trucks are tricky to turn on and off precisely, which makes flooded areas and dry spots more of a problem. And in the ones with gravity-feed watering systems, as the water in the tank decreases, the volume of water coming out decreases, leading to an inconsistent application of water.

Full water trucks hold a large amount of water, which can make for extremely heavy equipment driving over your footing. This can damage your base.

"One facility manager called me to problem-solve, and they had a 4,000-gallon water truck," Kiser says. "So that's 32,000 pounds of water, and a 35,000-pound truck. So he had probably 70,000 pounds that he was driving around the same track every time he watered the arena. They were getting areas where that truck went that got really hard, compared to the rest of the arena."

The only place where a water truck might be the best option is an outdoor arena in an arid climate like Arizona, Kiser says. And choose one that is smaller—2,000 gallon capacity, maximum.

Water Trailer

Another method is using a water trailer or wagon that attaches to your tractor or pickup. These allow for an easy and even distribution of water. Those who handle the equipment will need training to properly apply the water.

Kiser prefers this method of moisture application to most. He has customized and built water trailers that go from 300-gallon capacity up to 2,000 gallons.

"You have a lot better control of the water flow, you have lower volume, and you can control that

5.2 A water wagon or water tank on top of a drag implement is one of the most efficient methods of water application.

volume better," Kiser says. "You can choose a model with a sprayer for consistent water application."

Kiser's 2,000-gallon water trailer can dump a full tank in 10 minutes—faster than any other method, other than a water truck.

The downside is the cost of the implement, and the need for a tractor or truck to pull it.

Attwood says you can build a DIY version of a water wagon, with a water tank on a trailer and a PVC pipe with holes drilled into it. With the right connectors, water comes out the holes thanks to gravity. While this solution certainly is a budget option, Attwood notes it takes longer for the tank to empty. If your arena is at home and you aren't dealing with time constraints like you would be at a horse show, this may not be a downside.

"You're going to be going around the arena a lot more," Attwood says. "But in some ways, that's not a disaster, because often the longer it takes, the more evenly you can put the water out."

Randy Snodgress says another way to save money is by purchasing a smaller water trailer (smaller tank), but you'll end up having to refill more frequently, which will add to the time it takes to water your arena adequately, because it can take an hour to refill a water tank with a hose. If you refill from a pond or a tank with rainwater where you can refill quickly, a smaller water trailer can work well. He feels a water trailer, or a drag with a water tank on top of it—of any size—is preferable to other methods of applying water.

Cannon says a water tank on top of a drag implement is the most efficient method of water application, but depending on your water setup, if you lose pressure across the spray arm, it could lead to inconsistencies. This only happens with gravity-fed systems.

"It is the best way to get a large amount of water out in a short amount of time," she emphasizes.

Underground Methods

Several methods of underground watering systems have been developed that are ideal for arenas. Attwood says that while expensive, they work beautifully—better than most methods.

"The water comes up from underneath, and it's a very even amount of water that's getting added to the footing," Attwood says. "It's putting the water at the right place in the footing because you need the water at the bottom—you really don't need it at the top. You can also water while you're riding, and during a show. You don't need to stop the event to water the arena."

Ebb and Flow

Developed in Europe, this watering method is located underneath a top layer of sand, or sand and fiber, and the moisture bubbles up from below. When properly installed, this type of system delivers consistent moisture across the arena with little evaporation. The type of sand used is critical to its success and requires a specialist to install. It's also more expensive than other methods.

I mentioned Ebb and Flow earlier in these pages (see p. 76), but let's review how it works: Attwood says when you build an arena with this system, you install a plastic liner 18 inches down. Then you lay 4-inch pipes that are perforated with holes, followed by 8 inches of plain sand, and then 4 inches of your footing. (In Attwood's projects, the footing is sand mixed with textiles.) A round tank connected to both a water source and the underground pipes will be installed near the arena, and also to the pipes. When you fill up the tank with water, it will flow into the arena thanks to an adjustable valve system—think of the way a toilet works, Attwood explains. The method provides precision in how much water you have in your arena. It is an even way of watering the footing across the entire space at once. And when you have an Ebb and Flow system in an outdoor arena, Attwood says you can actually pump *out* water following a rainstorm to adjust the moisture content in the arena.

The main caveat to this type of watering system is the arena must be absolutely flat. Any slope at all will make for uneven moisture levels. Attwood also says this kind of system can lead to slightly less stable footing for the horse—he likens it to a waterbed because the bottom layer is saturated with water. In addition, the constant presence of water can lead to bacteria growing in the water.

This system must be carefully installed, or it will not work, Attwood warns.

ArenaWet™

This system is comprised of a series of "drip tubes" about 1 inch in diameter, built 2 feet apart into a rubber mat that sits underneath the sand footing in your arena. Each drip line has a valve every 12 inches that "weeps" moisture when water floods into the pipes. The system is set up in zones and connected to a sprinkler head control unit, so, similar to running a sprinkler system, you water each zone with a programmed timer.

> **EXPERT TIP**
>
> Bob Kiser says Ebb and Flow systems do not work for Western arenas with natural footing that require a hard base, such as cutting, reining, cow horse, or speed events. However, they can be considered for Western pleasure, trail, and Western riding.

"The footing gets wet, and the moisture travels by capillary action upward from the drip lines," Attwood explains. ArenaWet is expensive but works well, and is the method Attwood prefers. He says the rubber mats enhance the feel for horses riding over the surface, and riders enjoy the experience. "They can feel the cushion. It's not deep, but it's firm and has a bit of give. It's like wearing a great pair of running shoes."

The arena does not have to be perfectly level for this system—it can have a slope. This means installation is easier.

HIT Active-Aqua

This system is similar to the drip tubes of ArenaWet. You can save about 60 percent of water use, versus other methods such as sprinkler systems. This substantial water saving comes from the method the water is applied. Instead of watering from the top and hoping the water reaches the lower layer where you need the moisture, you're applying it directly to the lower layer. This reduces evaporation from the surface, so every bit of that moisture is being used.

You can also run moisture zones just where you need the water—say in a sunny area of an indoor arena that has dried out more quickly than other areas.

Finding the Right Moisture Balance

Proctor Test

Attwood says there is a method called a "Proctor test" to measure moisture in footing versus dry density. It is frequently used in the construction world.

"With this test, you take your footing, and you add moisture to it—let's say 10 beakers full of dry footing, and you add moisture to them all," Attwood says. "You add 8 percent, 10, 12, 14, 16, 18, 22, 24 percent moisture, and you mix them, then you try to compress it in a machine. And then you graph the results."

As the amount of water increases, that footing can be more compressed. At a certain point, you have too much moisture and it will need to drain. This can help inform your arena maintenance plan.

Comparative Weights

Another way Kiser measures moisture content in a footing mixture in his dirt lab is to place a sample of footing in a container and then weigh it. Then he microwaves the sample for three minutes. The moisture will evaporate. After shaking the mixture and letting it cool off, he'll microwave it again. He'll repeat the process until the footing is totally dry, and then weigh it again.

 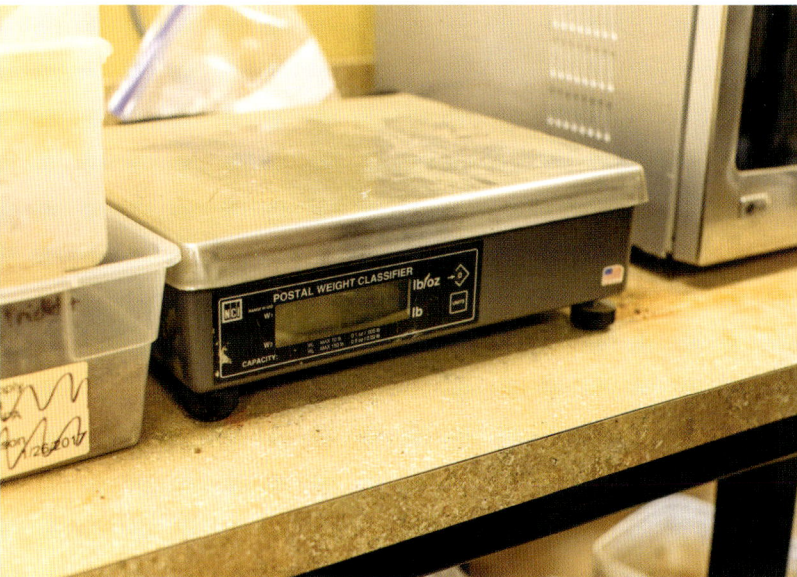

5.3 *In his dirt lab, Bob Kiser measures the ability of various footing mixtures to hold different amounts of water—helpful information when planning for maintenance of a particular arena. One method he uses is the "Proctor test," where he prepares a series of containers like this one, filled with footing, then adds different amounts of water to each container, and compresses them to see how much moisture the footing holds.*

5.4 *Kiser measures moisture content in a footing mixture by placing a sample of prepared footing in a container and weighing it, followed by microwaving the sample to evaporate the moisture. When the sample is completely dry, it is weighed again. From these two weights (before microwaving and after), he will calculate a moisture percentage for the footing.*

"You then have two weights for that footing," Kiser says. "Let's say it's 48 ounces [before microwaving] and 41.6 ounces [after]. That'll tell you what is your moisture percentage." (The difference is 6.4 ounces of water in the sample, which equates to 13.3 percent moisture.)

Moisture Meter

That level can also be measured using a moisture meter called a Field Scout®, which looks like a probe and can be used to test various points around your arena to help you gather information about how much more water you need to add. Attwood, Kiser, and

Moisture Management | 107

5.5 A–C *A moisture meter, like the Field Scout, is used to test moisture levels at various points around your arena. This information helps you know how much water to add to parts or the whole surface. The Field Scout has a probe at the end that gathers information from the footing material. You can walk around your arena and measure multiple points in the ground, and the Field Scout will give you an average moisture level reading, which helps you determine the amount of water to add.*

rodeo maintenance expert Randy Spraggins all use a moisture meter.

"That moisture meter is a really good investment for people who are really serious about preparing their surface to be the best it can," Attwood says. "So if they know it needs to be 16 percent moisture, they can easily walk around, measure 20 spots in the arena, and the instrument will give you an average moisture level on the screen. If it's 14 percent, you know you may need to add half a truckload of water to get it to the right amount of moisture."

For an at-home arena, a Field Scout may not be feasible, and your moisture needs may be different. After all, there are many factors that determine how much water you need, and how frequently you need to water, including climate, time of year, footing composition, usage, and more.

Hand Test

Another way to see how much moisture your arena has is to take a handful of the footing, squeeze it in your hand, and try to form a shape.

5.6 A–C Squeezing your footing by hand can provide information about its moisture level (A). You should be able to form a shape (B). If it doesn't hold together, the arena needs more water (C).

Moisture Management | 109

"If you can form a shape that will hold together, but is not a solid rock, that's not a bad place to start," Attwood says. "If it doesn't hold together, that's a sign that arena needs more water. Or the sand is incorrect. It does need to pack and hold together."

Observation

If your arena is getting dusty, Attwood says that's a good indicator it needs to be watered. Another sign is if the footing is not giving the right amount of support—if your horse is slipping around in the sand—it's time to add moisture.

"There isn't any way to put a quantity value on that," Kiser notes. "It's when can you recognize it needs to be watered. That's something you have to learn because your footing will be different than the arena down the road."

Moisture Needs Vary by Discipline

The type of riding being performed in your arena dictates how much moisture is needed. For example, Kiser says barrel horse ground needs to have a little bit of a firmer texture, like that used for hunter-jumpers.

"When they come into a barrel, you want it to give just a little bit, but not too much," Kiser says.

"Jumpers are similar—they have got to have really solid ground to push off of. You can call it 'purchase.' When they land, they also need a little bit of give."

Meanwhile, for cow horse events, they're looking for more moisture than say, reining, where you want your horse to be able to slide through the dirt.

"Maybe you'll stop a little shorter, but it'll hold

MOISTURE PERCENTAGES BY DISCIPLINE

The moisture percentage for most Western events should be in the 5 to 9 percent range, depending on the discipline, says Bob Kiser. Reining should be in the 5 percent area, 7 percent for cow horse, and 9 percent for barrel racing.

For the arenas Nick Attwood works with, the ideal amount of moisture is between 16 and 20 percent. The amount of moisture differs for each event. Attwood says dressage needs 16 percent, while jumping needs more water—18 to 20 percent.

For some upper-level English shows, Attwood notes, show managers have an idea of the percentage of moisture they want in the footing and will measure the moisture of the footing.

"With that information, they will know how much more water to add to get it to that perfect point."

5.7 How much moisture you need is dependent on the discipline you ride.

them better when they're on a cow," Kiser says. "But a little too much water, and a footing with some clay will get pretty sticky and pretty grabby. Add a little more water on an arena that is too sandy, and it'll give more resistance."

At a show such as the APHA World Show at Will Rogers Memorial Center in Fort Worth, Texas, Snodgress says switching from a class such as cutting, where the footing is deep and loose, to barrel racing, where the footing needs to be firmer, is possible with strategic amounts of water applied.

"I will put 6,000 to 8,000 gallons of water on that arena, and some riders might worry, thinking it's going to get slick, and if it had a lot of clay or silt in it, then it might get slick. But because it has so much sand, it just firms up with that water," Snodgress says.

For cow horse events, however, he notes there's a fine line between not enough moisture and too much.

"It can be too slick and give way when they set their back feet in the ground to stop and turn, or it can be too heavy, and without enough give when they set their back feet in the ground, which can injure them. In an arena with a lot of silt or clay, too much water can make it slippery. But not enough moisture can make it have too much give. Even for cutting, if it's too slippery, the horse can't get back to the cow quick enough."

For barrel racing, Leland Smith wants the arena to have enough moisture that there is no dust. He evaluates the moisture content by grabbing a handful of the dirt and squeezing it into a ball, as hard as he can.

"If I chunk it across the arena, and it hits and doesn't break up, I've got plenty of water," Smith says. "If it breaks into a couple of chunks, and doesn't fall apart, that's what I'm looking for."

This also depends on the composition of the footing. If you have more sand, you'll need more water.

"If you have sand, you can almost make mud out of it and horses will run better on it," Smith says. "If you have a lot of clay, you don't want that much water, because you'll end up having to run your ripper teeth [on your drag], and it packs a lot faster. We'll start adding some water if the dirt floats through the air, but we want it to flip up around their hocks and then lay right back down on the ground. We don't really want them to throw mud clods, but it depends on the dirt."

EXPERT TIP

If you're preparing to ride at offsite or competition arenas with footing that is heavier or looser than what you have currently at home, Randy Snodgress recommends making adjustments to the moisture content in your training arena to help your horse acclimate.

ADDITIVES THAT AFFECT MOISTURE

In chapter 3, we discussed oils, waxes, and polymer coatings (see p. 62). These additives all reduce or eliminate the need for added water.

Another method of moisture management that does not use water is *magnesium chloride*. This is a salt derivative that draws moisture from the air. It is applied as flakes or pellets onto your footing, and those flakes or pellets absorb moisture from the atmosphere to help keep your arena moist. Magnesium chloride has been used on roads and highways in the past to prevent dust or ice.

This product works well to keep arenas moist in humid climates, but is less effective in arid climates, Kiser says.

Attwood adds that it works well in climates where freezing temperatures make applying water difficult. It will also keep your footing from freezing until temperatures reach a much lower temperature.

"There is a reaction with the soil that bonds the soil together," Kiser says. "Plus it keeps the moisture in, so you don't have to water. It keeps the dust down, draws moisture in and will make the ground compact more."

One downside is when magnesium chloride is used in an outdoor arena, heavy rainfall can wash the salt product into groundwater.

Attwood says the product also dissipates over time and will need to be applied every year.

"The more magnesium chloride you add, the better the footing will be; however, the more caustic it will be," Attwood says. "You can end up adding too much, and it'll be detrimental to the health of your horse."

While this product does work, Kiser does not advise using it. If you do, he says make sure to get it from a reliable source. Otherwise, you could end up with saltwater brine from oil wells, for example.

"I don't recommend using magnesium chloride," he notes. "It's corrosive. You'd need to wash your horse's feet and make sure it's picked out because it's not only that it's corrosive—it'll suck the moisture right out of your horse's feet."

In addition to damaging your horse's hooves, Snodgress adds the product can corrode pipe fences, metal drag equipment, and other items in the arena. He says the cost of applying magnesium chloride once every six months may be better invested in a decent water trailer.

Time of Year and Climate

If you have an outdoor arena, you'll generally need more water in the summer than in the winter.

"You have to learn to judge the humidity, too," Kiser says. "Outdoor arenas, that makes a huge difference. Even indoors, it will have an effect."

And when the temperatures dip below freezing, adding water can be challenging. You don't want your watering method to freeze, and you also don't want your top layer of footing to freeze. In colder climates, *Equestrian Surfaces* suggests watering thoroughly in the fall to prepare the footing as best you can before temperatures drop. (You might also consider adding salt to your footing—magnesium chloride. But do so with caution—see sidebar, p. 113.)

The rule? Moisture is very climate- and season-dependent. For example, watering an arena in Texas with 1,000 gallons of water, three or four days a week will turn your arena into a mud bowl in the winter, Kiser says. But in July? That probably won't be enough water.

Watering Routine

Water your arena first, and then drag it, Kiser says. At a personal arena, versus a horse show facility, he recommends watering late in the evening and letting it sit overnight, before dragging in the morning.

"Water will draw other moisture from the air," he explains. "Your arena will actually be a little bit wetter because the water had a chance to soak in all night before you dragged it. It had time to soak through the soil profile, which is ideal."

As discussed earlier in this chapter, you can also use a drag implement outfitted with a water tank, where the water sprays *in front* of the drag tools. Kiser recommends avoiding a tool that drags and then waters behind it.

"That way, your water is just lying on top of the ground," Kiser says. "You have to incorporate that moisture. Otherwise, it won't last as long. It'll evaporate a lot faster."

In addition to watering equipment, you'll also need other maintenance equipment to groom your arena footing. We'll discuss these implements in the next chapter.

CHAPTER 6
ARENA MAINTENANCE EQUIPMENT

When you've invested time and money into building an arena with good footing, or when you are committed to improving the footing or arena you already have, working with suitable equipment is a vital piece of the puzzle. The correct tools will allow maintenance of your arena to be more efficient and effective.

There are many pieces of equipment to choose from, some better suited to the job than others. To avoid spending more money than necessary and still purchase the best equipment for the job, researching these various tools and methods is important.

This chapter will outline some basic categories of equipment you will want to invest in to maintain your arena. We'll discuss what features are necessary and what are simply nice to have. The price points for arena equipment span a huge range. It's my hope to give you some guidance on what you need as you prepare to invest in equipment.

Choosing Equipment

Evaluate your ground and determine what kind of equipment best suits your particular arena and needs, Randy Snodgress says. For example, a mostly sand arena can get by with a lower-end drag, but one with higher clay content will need a step up in equipment.

"You need to know what kind of material you have, and then research what kind of drag is going to work with that material," Snodgress advises. "And make sure your tractor has enough horsepower to effectively pull that drag."

He recommends finding others with arena footing similar to yours, who are doing the same discipline as you, and find out what kind of equipment they are using. Are they happy with it? Would they change anything about it?

David Detweiler owns Carolina Arena Company and has supplied equipment for many major English

events. He recommends starting by looking at entry-level models of equipment to see if they will perform as you need them to. Avoid selecting the cheapest model as your default.

"Your equipment is probably one of the most important things, especially after you've spent a lot of money on your footing," Detweiler says. "People will spend $100,000 on footing and then get a piece of equipment for less than $2,000 and try to maintain it. You're not going to be able to get the value of your riding on that footing if you don't use the proper equipment to maintain it."

Equipment Basics

Here are the minimum tools you need to maintain an arena with footing comprised of *natural materials* (sand, silt, clay, sandy loam):

6.1 Getting the right equipment—including the right tractors, drags, and waterers—to maintain your arena and your footing is crucial to your arena's longevity and a horse's ability to safely train and perform on it.

- A drag that levels, loosens the soil, rips to deepen the footing when needed, adjusts the depth, and smooths the surface.

- A water trailer or other method to water your arena.

- An angle blade to bring in dirt from arena edges.

- A roller to "seal" an outdoor arena from rain.

- A tractor that is powerful enough to do the job now and in the future.

Here are tools you'll need to maintain an arena that includes *synthetic/non-natural materials* (wax-coated sand, fiber, rubber):

- A drag that levels the top footing and has the capability to loosen footing when needed.

- Watering method (see chapter 5—p. 97).

Drag

This is probably the most important tool you'll buy for your arena, and the options can be overwhelming, especially if you're budget-conscious. But that money is very well-spent. Consider how much money you've sunk into your arena. If you don't purchase a good drag to maintain it, you will not get the best use out

6.2 A & B Choose a drag designed to maintain surfaces for your chosen discipline—and make sure it is made for the type of footing you have. Here are two types and sizes, with water tanks incorporated, as some of our experts recommend.

Arena Maintenance Equipment | **117**

of your investment in your arena. In fact, it could end up worse off due to improper maintenance.

Bob Kiser says in general, the bigger the drag you can buy and the bigger the tractor you can pull it with, the better results you'll see. But that's not feasible for everyone—so ultimately, you need to get the most for what you can afford.

He's not a proponent of choosing a drag so small that it can be pulled behind a four-wheeler. From his perspective, they don't do an adequate job preparing the footing, and they'll take many more passes around the arena than a bigger drag. (His company is working on developing scaled-down versions of the premier drags offered.)

Kiser says there are three main US-based companies that manufacture arena drags made for natural material footing: ABI Arena Drag, Kiser Ranch Development, and Snodgress's ArenaWerks.

"All of them have slightly different features, but the end result is similar because they're all designed with the same processes," Kiser says. "If you're really serious and you've got a training operation in the Western disciplines (except for the barrel horse industry), those are the three drags you need to pick from."

6.3 A leveling blade is an important feature to your drag tool.

Purpose of a Drag

For an arena made with natural materials (sand, silt, and clay—not fiber or rubber mix), your drag needs to, first of all, level the arena. Some drag tools use an automated laser system where the blade automatically adjusts to level the arena.

"If you've got a reining horse arena, and a clay base, and your sand is 3 inches deep, what happens if that sand starts moving toward the end where your fence is?" Kiser says. "Where it came from is now 2 inches deep…. That's why it's critical for your drag to be able to bring that sand back where it belongs. Otherwise your arena is not consistent."

You don't necessarily need a laser system, Kiser

says, although it's preferable. Many pull-type drags can keep the ground fairly level, although three-point-hitch drags are more problematic.

"A three-point hitch drag is notorious about causing the ground to get uneven because you don't have enough ground plane from various points to keep the drag running level," he explains. "The only place where they work well is in barrel horse arenas, and they're used a lot for those arenas because they maneuver easily."

Behind your leveling blade, the drag should be able to loosen the soil up and remove your tractor tire tracks as its second step. And the third step is "rippers"—blades that can address how deep your ground is.

"We don't use rippers very often, but we do once in a while," Kiser says. "They are something you really do need to have. The only exception is if you've got an indoor arena with a clay base with sand on it. I tell people to take the rippers out [of their drag] because, inevitably, someday, they're going to get let down, and it'll damage the base."

Your drag needs a method of depth control. Some drags can be adjusted hydraulically to change up the depth.

"That is one of the most important things, because if you don't have a way to control the

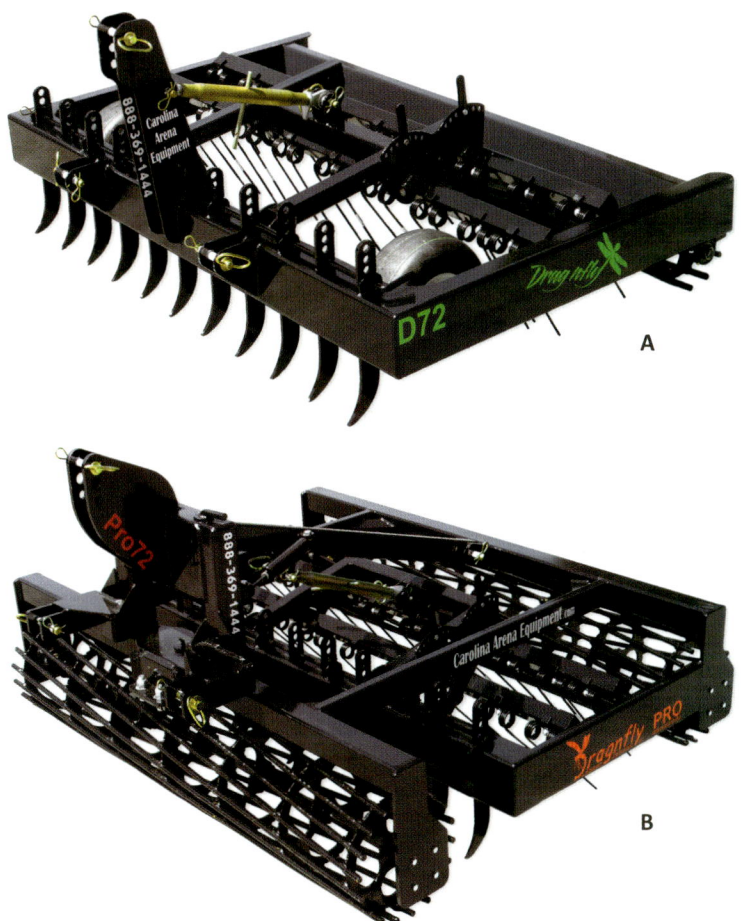

6.4 A & B *For arenas with textiles or other synthetic materials blended with sand, your drag needs to be able to keep the footing at the right mixture, like this example from the Drag-Nfly brand (A). Some drags, include a bar roller to control ripper teeth depth (B).*

Arena Maintenance Equipment | 119

depth, you can't do a good job of dragging the arena," Kiser notes.

For an arena with textiles or other materials mixed with sand, your drag needs to help keep the footing at the right mixture, says David Detweiler.

"When you have a training facility where you have 10 to 30 horses out riding across the arena, it's pounding down on the footing and it's going to separate somewhat," he explains. "Your bigger materials are going to come to the top, and the finer materials will fall down. If you don't have the proper equipment to keep it at the right mixture, it's going to separate and it's not going to do what it's supposed to."

After a final cut of your material, smoothing out the base, the goal is to get your arena to where every square inch of the footing is exactly the same. This is followed by a finishing device to put a nice finish on the footing.

Water Trucks or Trailers

We already discussed moisture management in depth (see p. 93), but of those systems mentioned, two are potential pieces of arena management equipment: a water truck and a water trailer. The consensus of our experts is that a water trailer or wagon is the preferable implement, so I'll focus on that here.

Kiser is such a proponent of a water trailer that he has customized and manufactures several versions of this tool.

"If I thought there was a better way to water an arena, I'd be selling that," he says. "I think overall, it's the best way for the average person to water their arena."

You can pull a water trailer with a pickup truck or a tractor. Kiser advises using a tractor if you have it because trailers are more maneuverable behind a tractor, and you don't need a huge tractor to do it.

"You can pull a 1,000-gallon water trailer with about a 50-horsepower tractor," he says.

If you choose a smaller water trailer, like a 500-gallon model, you can even pull it with a UTV such as a Gator™. A caution though—don't pull a water wagon down a hill with such a vehicle or you're liable to get run over.

Regardless of which model you choose, Kiser recommends one with either a manual or electric valve that allows you to turn the water on and off from your towing vehicle.

"There are some where you have to turn the valve

> **EXPERT TIP**
>
> For a barrel racing pen, many prefer a drag tool called the Black Widow Groomer, which rips and also compacts the soil with a rolling basket. Leland Smith, who specializes in barrel racing footing, prefers a drag with hydraulic ripper teeth, and a blade to level, and a roller on the back to break up dirt clods.

on before you get on the tractor, and leave it on until you are done watering and get off the tractor to turn it off. You'll notice when you water an arena, the ends can get watered five times more than the rest of the arena if you can't shut it off from the driver's seat."

A low-cost solution to this issue is a ratchet valve on the back of the water pump with a rope attached. You can pull the rope, and it'll turn the valve a quarter-turn, and snap back to open it. Pull it again and it'll turn another quarter-turn to shut it off.

"That's the least expensive way," Kiser says. "The electric valves are quite a bit more expensive, but they're a lot nicer to operate."

For a budget option when it comes to water trucks and trailers, Snodgress says you can experiment with putting a water storage container on the back of your pickup truck, and attach a PVC pipe with holes drilled into it to rain water onto the ground—just make sure to build in a valve to turn it on and off.

Tractors

When considering potential tractors, keep the following tips in mind:

Front-Wheel Assist: The most important feature you need on a tractor is front-wheel assist, Kiser says. "Do not under any circumstances buy a two-wheel drive tractor to pull the larger drags," he emphasizes. "Two-wheel drives will displace footing when you turn."

However, do not drive the tractor in four-wheel drive outside the arena. "The minute you drive out of the arena, take it out of four-wheel drive," Kiser says. "That's really hard on the powertrain and on the tires to drive on hard surfaces in four-wheel drive."

Buy Bigger: Aim to buy a slightly bigger or more powerful tractor than what you think you'll need, and "Always overpower yourself a little bit," as Kiser says. This is for several reasons. Maybe today you can only afford to purchase a light-duty drag, so you buy a 30-horsepower tractor. But if in two years, you've acquired more horses, you have more money to spend, and you want to upgrade to a bigger drag—you can't pull a bigger drag with the tractor you have. But if you had bought a 60-horsepower tractor, you could easily upgrade the drag and still be able to pull it with your tractor.

Snodgress says options range from a lawn mower to a 100-plus horsepower tractor. The same vehicle, just like the same drag, does not work for every situation.

Another element to consider is the size of your arena. Detweiler says a large tractor will save time dragging a large arena but may not be maneuverable in a small arena. In that situation, you *should* consider

6.5 A & B Choosing the right tractor and drag equipment can make maintaining and preserving your arena much easier, while saving you valuable time. Aim to purchase a slightly bigger or more powerful tractor than you think you'll need. Here we see John Deere (A) and Kubota (B) examples.

a smaller, more compact tractor. "In a smaller ring, you want a smaller tractor," he says. "With a big tractor, you won't have enough room to maneuver, and if there are jumps in there, you can hit the jumps."

Remote Hydraulics: No matter which tractor you select, Kiser recommends buying two sets of remote hydraulics—this will pair well with drags that have remote hydraulic cylinders. On a smaller tractor, this is an add-on option. On larger tractors over 90 horsepower, they are standard. Remote hydraulic outlets allow you to operate hydraulic cyclinders. When you purchase the hydraulics at the time you buy the tractor, the cost is much lower than adding them on later.

Tires: Kiser prefers R4 tires, which is an industrial-type tire versus deep lug tires. "They work better in a horse arena versus the deeper lug tractor tires made for farm work," he says. "But if you're getting a 45-horsepower tractor, don't get the R1s, get the R4s."

Avoid Front-End Loaders: If your tractor has one, take the time to remove the bucket or forks before dragging your arena. "They are dangerous," Kiser says. "With a front-end loader sticking out in front of you while you're dragging an arena, if you're not paying attention, it can hook a fence, a gate, a wall, or a beam. It's something else you're focusing on when you should be looking backward at your arena drag."

Amenities: After the basic requirements, you can choose from a host of tractor amenities and features to make your job a little easier.

Whether or not you choose a tractor with a *cab* is personal preference. Kiser prefers a tractor without so he has better visibility of the drag process. "I would rather not have a cab on a tractor because the visibility is not near as good," Kiser says. "The glass can give you a little distortion when you're looking behind you. But if you're using that tractor on a farm or ranch, and you're going out and hauling hay when its 10 below zero with the wind blowing—it's a matter of what else you're using that tractor for."

If you don't have a front-end loader (which Kiser says to avoid), you'll want to add some weights on the front of the tractor. This is to counteract the weight of the drag you're pulling.

Other Tools
Drum Roller
Outdoor arenas can benefit from being smoothed off and sealed prior to heavy rains. Kiser says to do this, you can use a small "drum roller" if you want to make that investment, or you can take a larger arena drag

and raise it till the blade is just touching the ground. This will smooth and compact the footing so it won't soak up excess water.

"A smooth drum roller is ideal, but if you've got a good arena drag you can run it right on top of the ground," Kiser says. "You're trying to get all the hoof prints and tire tracks out so that the arena will shed water."

Another option that can work to "seal off" your arena prior to rainfall is to attach a gate, or a length of chain link fence to your tractor.

"Anything that will make your footing really smooth," Snodgress says. "You could use a three-point grader blade and turn it around to do the same thing."

For footing with textiles in the mix, the equipment you use needs to keep the footing at the right compaction. This could be smooth drum rollers that give the footing a finished, carpeted look. If you're not using the footing for a season, Detweiler recommends using a solid roller to "close it up" and seal it off.

"That helps protect your footing when you're not using it, or before a big rainstorm," Detweiler says.

EXPERT TIP

If you have a pipe and cable fence around your arena, you may need a short blade that you attach to your tractor and back under the fence in each section to pull out the sand.

Angle Blade

If your drag can't pull sand off the edges of your arena, you'll want to get an angle blade tool to attach to your tractor to go around and roll the sand back into the arena. Kiser says many drag implements have this feature attached to the corner of the drag, but if not, you do need to purchase an additional tool.

Hand Tools

Shovel: If you have a no-climb wire fence or some other fencing designs where even a short angle blade can't be used, you'll have to resort to moving sand off the edges of the arena by by hand.

Manure Rake: Detweiler says every arena needs a manure rake handy to scoop up manure before you drag. "Manure can create bacteria and problems in your footing. Try to keep any horse manure off your footing as much as possible. You *do not* want to drag on top of manure and mix it into your footing."

Tools to Avoid

- Both Kiser and Snodgress advise against using a *disc rototiller* on your arena. "They're not intended to use on an arena, and they'll cut grooves into your ground," Kiser says. "They are made to get your fields ready to plant crops."

- Do not use a *power harrow* or a *box blade*. Kiser says some folks try to address a hard arena surface with a box blade and the rippers pointing down, but there's no way to control the depth and it can ruin the base.

- For an arena with a fiber mixture, Detweiler says you should not use a *leveling blade*. Note: This is the only footing material where you don't want a leveler. "You cannot use a leveling device on fiber mixtures because it will clump up and separate your footing," he says.

Maintaining Your Equipment

To protect your investment in your equipment, regular maintenance of that equipment is important. Kiser says he takes pride in his equipment and that means taking care of it. This requires addressing issues *before* implements break and damage your arena.

If you're not mechanically inclined—or if you're unfamiliar with your equipment—read the owner's manuals carefully. When your equipment does not have a manual, ask your equipment dealers for advice. Kiser says he has a mobile mechanic service to help customers keep their tools in good working condition.

"My background was in farming—that's all I did," Kiser says. "You either took care of your equipment, or you went broke. Those were the two options, because you can't let your equipment break when you're farming."

Tractor

"I recommend checking the fluids on a tractor every day," Kiser says. "On new tractors, that's pretty simple.

MAINTENANCE QUICK REFERENCE CHECKLIST

TRACTOR
- Change the oil.
- Check and change air filters.
- Check hydraulic fluid.
- Check air pressure and condition on tires.
- Check water and connections in battery.
- Check water level in radiator.

DRAG
- Check grease and wheel bearings.
- Check ripper teeth and part of the drag that contacts the footing.
- Check air pressure and condition on tires.

You've got a dipstick in your oil pan so that's easy to do. Check to see if you've got engine oil. Check the water level in the radiator—it's usually a clear plastic container and easy to see. Even the hydraulics on the back will have a sight tune that easy to check. If not, you've usually got a dipstick."

Read your owner's manual to see how frequently you need to change your oil, filters, and hydraulic oil.

Water Trailer

Kiser recommends draining water trailers on the first day of November—or before your first freeze, depending on where you live. Otherwise, your water pump, pipes, and shutoff valves could break from freezing. If you know it's going to freeze, drain your water trailer.

Don't leave water sitting in a white water tank—Kiser says it'll grow algae, which can destroy the water pumps when you do water your arena. Black tanks don't have the same issue.

Now that we've discussed the necessary equipment to care for your arena, in the next chapter I'll go over in detail how to do that maintenance.

CHAPTER 7

ARENA GROOMING AND MAINTENANCE

Every arena, from the most beautiful competition space to a backyard riding ring, needs proper maintenance to be usable for horses. While specifics vary based on usage, type of riding on the surface, climate, and composition of the footing, according to *Equestrian Surfaces,* your maintenance should strive for a number of goals:

- A consistent and even top layer.
- A good ratio of materials in the mixture.
- A looser top layer without compaction.
- Consistent and correct moisture.
- Protection for the base and middle layers.
- No manure in the arena.

Nick Attwood says his goal for arena maintenance is to create a surface that has all the right properties: *firmness, grippiness,* and *responsiveness.*

"You are dialing into these properties for the footing, and you want to make it consistent as well," he advises.

Bob Kiser says arena maintenance should address two main goals, and both of them involve safety: "Safety of the rider and safety of the horse, those should be your major concerns."

EXPERT TIP

Oklahoma City's Fairgrounds arenas have a concrete foundation, with a good 15 inches of sand/silt/clay mixture on top. When Kiser Ranch Development is maintaining those arenas for horse shows, Kiser uses water and drag equipment to compact a hard pan and then works up the top layer to be the right consistency for each event. The depth of the top layer and moisture content change for each event.

Kiser says a concave profile blade on the drag equipment creates the hard pan by packing down the lower layer of footing, removing ridges from the footing that could cause a horse to be injured.

With improperly maintained footing, the risk for injuries—and worse, fatalities—of horse and rider increases.

Like Kiser, Randy Snodgress has two main goals in arena maintenance: to keep the footing as safe and consistent as possible.

Regular Maintenance Techniques

Go for a Walk

Whether you are your own maintenance crew or a rider—or both—Kiser recommends spending time each day walking on your arena footing.

"I can go to an arena, and walk across it, and I can tell you about what needs to be done," Kiser says. "You can feel where there's a spot where the ground is a little bit softer. That means there's a hole in the base, or something is wrong there. You can continue walking along and it gets really solid, because you're not going down into the dirt very much. That tells you the footing is not very deep."

Kiser walks around arenas carrying a flat-nose shovel, and he uses it like a cane.

"I just keep sticking that shovel in the ground as I'm walking to see what it feels like, when I'm looking at someone's arena to advise them," he says.

MAINTENANCE CREW

The person maintaining your arena has a critical job in preserving your investment in the arena itself, as well as your horse. Make sure this person has adequate training on how to maintain the arena, as well as enough time to do the job correctly. Whenever possible, your maintenance team could include more than one person, as top-quality arenas require a significant amount of regular maintenance.

If you feel like one spot is a little sandier, or there's a hole, that can be dangerous. You want the footing to be as consistent as possible across the arena in all areas. When you struggle to walk across your arena, that's a sign something needs to be changed about the footing. Maybe it's too deep, maybe it needs more moisture or maybe the composition of the footing is incorrect.

"You shouldn't have trouble walking in the arena," Kiser says. "That's why I always preach don't just ride in your arena. Walk across it, see what it really feels like."

Drag Speed

Make sure you're dragging at a reasonable speed. Snodgress says you can't make really good quality ground quickly. Dragging too fast can cause your tractor and drag to bounce out of the dirt and throw footing to the outside of the arena. The safety of the horse and rider depends on the arena footing, Snodgress warns. That's why it's important not to rush that care.

"You want that drag to be able to get in the arena and work, and keep the depth that you want so you don't have to go super slow, either," Snodgress says. "Our general rule of thumb is somewhere between 5 and 6 miles per hour, because the bit going out around the edges will smooth out a little bit better. If we need to do some fixing of the footing, we'll slow down to maybe 4½ miles an hour so we can pay a little bit more attention."

Drag Patterns

The path you take to drag your arena doesn't have to be complicated, and you don't have to overdo it. Kiser says if your drag doesn't level at the same time as it drags, it'll make any uneven areas worse the more you drag.

"I basically only use two patterns, and they're the same standard pattern that I use at a horse show," Kiser says.

Kiser recommends alternating the direction in which you start your drag pattern. "If you went to the right this time, next time go to the left. So change the pattern that way."

Some arena drag manufacturers recommend a technique called "spin it out" where you drag in concentric circles. Kiser says this will push the dirt out to the perimeter, and he does not recommend this pattern. Instead, make ovals. Avoid coming right up to the wall or fence when you make turns during your drag time. Instead, make one last pass close to the wall before you leave the arena.

For barrel racing, Leland Smith changes directions every time he drags, even when it is a quick drag around the cloverleaf pattern in between runs.

"We're grabbing dirt and putting it in holes, and if we keep going in the same direction, it's just going to make your hole move across the arena," Smith says. "So you turn around the next drag, every five or three horses, and you go the opposite direction to bring that dirt back the other direction. You're changing directions, doing small circles, ripping it diagonally, just changing the dirt every time. You can't stay in the same pattern or your arena will become uneven and may get waves in it."

Snodgress says you should avoid dragging the exact same route every day. "You don't realize that

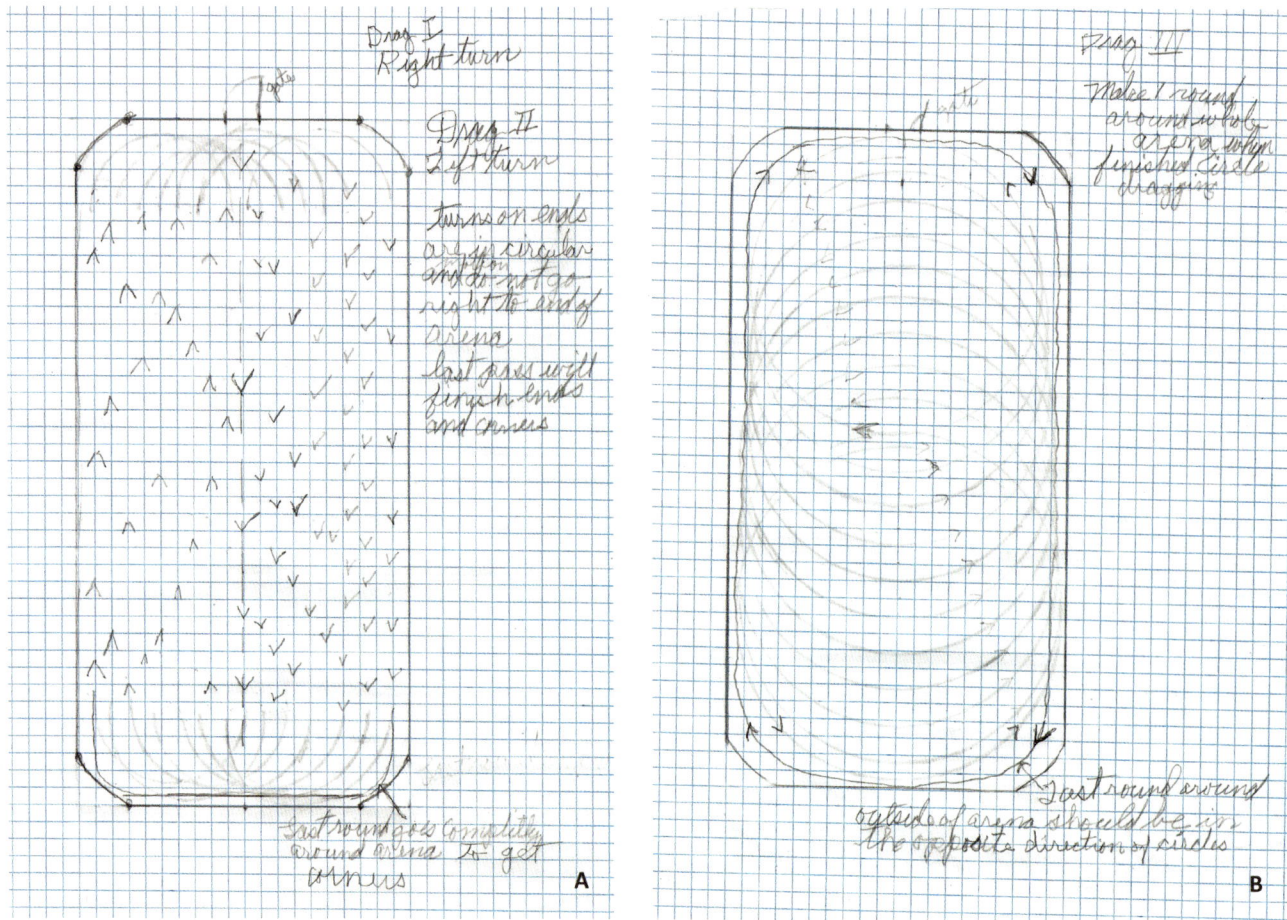

7.1 A & B *Kiser uses two patterns in his maintenance of Western performance horse arenas at horse shows. In one of them, you alternate the direction you go each time you drag (A). In the other, you make continuous circles, followed by one complete round of the arena (B). Note: These patterns are recommended for most Western events, with the exception of barrel racing.*

when you turn the tractor, it'll roll a little bit like a car does. It will lean through the curves. Even if it's just an eighth of an inch, if you do that in the same spot every day for a year, you are going to create a hole there. That's how you get rolls and waves in an arena."

Instead, go down the middle of the arena and turn to the left some days and then go to the right the other days in a week. Circle from one end of your arena and then the other.

"Work the arena in different directions, so you're moving that dirt different ways, instead of moving all the time in the exact same spots and creating problems," Snodgress advises.

David Detweiler says when maintaining an arena with synthetic materials such as fiber, you must vary the patterns you drag.

"It's very, very important if you have synthetic footing to not follow the same drag pattern every time you drag," Detweiler says. "You have to go in different directions, you can do circle motions one way and then do circles the other way the next time. That way it keeps your arena a lot more level."

Water

As we covered in chapter 5 (p. 93), how often you water depends on a lot of factors, but the climate and temperature are two that have a big impact. Also, whether your ring is outdoor, covered, or indoor. For example, an indoor arena experiences less evaporation than an outdoor. But a heated indoor arena has more evaporation than an unheated one.

An arena surface comprised of sand, felt, and fiber requires much less maintenance than some other combinations, but Attwood says it still needs care—particularly in adding the right amount of moisture.

"When there's moisture in the footing, fibers tend to stay incorporated into the sand," he says. "If you let the sand get too dry, and there's no moisture in it, the fibers will come to the surface."

If the footing gets too dry, you'll need to add moisture back to the sand and it needs to be conditioned with an implement that has teeth to reincorporate the textiles back into the sand. The longer you allow fiber and sand to separate, the more difficult it is to remix. Too much moisture, like when an arena gets flooded from heavy rain, also causes fibers to float to the surface. This will also require conscientious dragging to remix the materials once the footing has gotten a little drier.

EXPERT TIP

Sometimes an arena needs more moisture when switching from one event to another. Cutting is one event where the moisture content needs to be higher than most other Western events. That's why a water tank on top of a drag can be a real benefit, particularly at a horse show.

CASE STUDY

LAZY E ARENA

The Lazy E Arena in Guthrie, Oklahoma, is home to many major rodeo and barrel events, including the Pink and Ruby Buckle races, the Barrel Futurities of America World Championships, and the Lance Graves International race. Leland Smith does maintenance for several barrel events at this arena. Preparing ground for barrel racing events is his specialty.

At a barrel race, the ground crew will drag around the cloverleaf three-barrel pattern every few horses, and do a "big drag" at a larger interval. For each set of horses, the "top of the ground" is right after the big drag and "bottom of the ground" is right before the next drag. Typically, riders prefer to be out first since that is when the footing is most even.

"What we try to do for barrel racing is make sure we apply moisture, and we want the dirt to hold," Smith says. "The problem is you'll have 700 horses running in one day, and some of them went on top of the ground. Some of them go in there and bury their butts in the dirt. It's so many different horses. So, you've got to try to find a happy medium."

Smith adds moisture in the footing, rips the footing deeply and puts it back together on top of a firmer base, aiming for footing holding together to support the horses as they run and turn at top speed.

Managing barrel racing footing is challenging under the best of circumstances. When performances come down to differences of thousandths of a second, and a horse or rider can be severely injured—or worse—from a fall, good, safe, consistent ground is critical.

"I've seen horses break legs, break hips," Smith says. "Accidents happen, and a lot of times it has nothing to do with the dirt or the tractor drivers. We try hard to keep all of the horses and riders safe while making it as competitive as possible. We want it to be fast, but we want it to be safe, too."

"We'll put the teeth [of the implement] into the footing, maybe 3 inches deep, trying to get as deep as we can, and turn that footing over, going round and round the arena for hours to reincorporate it," Attwood says. "Once you feel you've got it reincorporated, you'll wind the teeth up to only drag around an inch and a half, so you can get the bottom layer knitted together. You don't want 3 inches of fluff; it'll be too much."

Primary Maintenance Routines

Dragging for a Horse Show

Attwood says for an English-discipline horse show at arenas his team has managed, the maintenance crew starts early, making sure to apply the right amount of moisture before the show begins, before any fences are set up, and before any dressage rings are in place. This is also the time to get the arena perfectly dragged.

"If you don't do that, it will get away from you, especially if you're doing it in the summer," Attwood says. "The moisture level is critical to all of these properties. So you want to start with the arena at the right level of moisture, and then your job is to top up what you're losing to evaporation."

During a show's long days, Attwood says maintenance crews will water often—usually with water trucks.

"They're massive arenas, too big for sprinkler systems," he says. "We'll water if it's hot or windy. When the show finishes at night, we'll put a few loads of water onto the surface, and then we'll come back in the morning and put more water on it if it's required, and we'll drag before the horses appear."

Maintaining an arena during an event is challenging because the maintenance crew has to work with show management and exhibitors to have enough time to do what's needed to keep the footing in top shape.

"There'll be breaks where you can water and drag, and everything needs to be well-coordinated because you may only get 20 minutes, an hour at lunchtime, and depending on how many arenas you're looking after, you've got to get in them as soon as you can," Attwood says. "Your access to the arenas is really limited during the day."

Dragging for a Training Arena

For most backyard or boarding arenas, dragging once a day is sufficient. Kiser says if you're only riding one or two horses, you can get by with dragging every other day, unless you need to water.

"For all-around horses, you can probably ride 25 or 30 horses before you really need to drag again," he

says. "[As compared to] reining, at one of those big facilities with two or three trainers—they'll drag three times a day."

Snodgress also recommends dragging frequently. Dragging your footing lifts the top layer and adds air to it, increasing the cushion. As the dirt sits overnight, it'll settle and get firmer. Dragging infrequently (say, once a week), can also allow grass and weeds to gain a foothold—something Snodgress says is a challenge to any good arena.

"They're a nightmare because they make everything ball up under your drag, and you can't make the arena look nice," Snodgress says. "So you really need to drag at least once a day."

You can drag more than that when you see inconsistencies in the dirt. When there are lots of footprints, sliding-stop tracks, overworked areas, or dirt is getting pitted around a barrel or jump it's time to drag.

7.2 Reining footing needs to be able to hold up to horses circling at speed without slipping, but the top layer needs to be loose enough to allow the horse to slide during stops. When a facility has a large number of horses training in an arena, they may have to drag several times a day.

7.3 An arena being used for jumping needs to be dragged when the footing around the jumps gets pitted or overworked.

Arena Grooming and Maintenance | 135

Arena Care Don'ts

Don't Use Your Arena as a Turnout

An arena, especially an indoor, can be a tempting space for turnout because it's often a safe, large enclosure, perhaps even covered in inclement weather. But turning a horse out in an arena means you'll have significantly more manure ground into the footing, and if you feed your horse grain or hay while turned out, those hay stalks can also mix into the material.

Feeding hay in an arena is one of Kiser's biggest pet peeves when it comes to arena care.

"It's the worst thing you can do," Kiser says. "You throw it in one spot, so now you have a pile of hay in there that's going to get caught up in your drag, and it's a mess."

7.4 Arena footing with fiber additives, like this one, needs less maintenance than some other footings, but it may need extra moisture added or to be remixed to keep the fibers incorporated.

LONG-TERM MAINTENANCE

Besides adding water and dragging your arena on a regular basis, periodically you may want to re-grade the footing. Attwood says some serious training facilities re-level and laser grade their arenas several times a year.

"A lot of our clients schedule us to come back either annually or biannually to bring our laser grading equipment," Attwood says. "That basically levels the arena and makes it perfect again."

Attwood also recommends that every three or four years you scrape off all the footing to mix, blend, and re-lay your base.

"This has the benefit of taking away any inconsistencies in the arena that could potentially happen, [for example] because riders are constantly riding around the perimeter so it's getting more wear and tear," Attwood says. "Over time, arena footing will get more and more compact and the air in the footing disappears slowly. If the footing is freshly laid and set in place, that adds a bit of air to it, and maintains its longevity."

During this process, Attwood will take a sample of the footing to his lab to see if it needs more textiles (when that is a component), or if the horses have broken down the fiber. That way, more fiber can be added and the footing can be reformulated before it is laid back down.

7.5 Manure accumulations contribute to poor arena conditions. They will degrade the footing mixture and add bacteria.

Tying your horse along the arena rail is not good for the arena either, Kiser notes. This will damage your footing in that area in more ways than one.

"They'll leave manure everywhere, and worse, they'll paw at the ground," Kiser says.

Don't Let Manure Accumulate

Poop happens, but that doesn't mean you should let horse manure pile up in your arena. Attwood says besides contributing to bacteria in the arena, manure accumulations break down into dust. When you've paid for a dust-free pen like a wax-covered sand footing, this defeats one of the biggest benefits to that footing choice.

Kiser says manure is one of the bigger enemies to a horse arena. Even if it degrades to becoming invisible, the hay your horse digested will remain in the footing.

"You get enough organic matter, and the footing

will start to pack more," Kiser says. "Especially if you get too much moisture on your footing, that organic material from the manure will cause the footing to really bond together."

Adding stall shavings and manure is even more detrimental.

"Some people will do that if the ground gets to packing down too hard, and they put some shavings in it," Kiser says. "Yeah it works, but it isn't too long till they've got a real mess in there that goes to decomposing, and you get an unpleasant dust out of it, that's just not something you want to do."

Don't Longe in the Same Spot

Longing is an important part of many riding and training programs, but it can wreak havoc on your footing. The repetitive tight circles with a handler in the center can carve deep into the material, making grooves and resulting in an uneven surface.

If you have to longe your horse, do it in a round pen if one is available. If that is not possible, and your arena is where you prefer to longe, move your circles each time you do it. The same goes for jumps, stops, spins, pirouettes, barrel turns, and other repetitive exercises. Whenever possible, change up where you do these moves so they happen in different parts of the arena to help keep your footing in its place.

"Protect yourself a little bit—move over 10 feet when you're spinning [for example] so you don't make the center of the arena too deep," Kiser says. "It's the worst thing you can do—circling on a line and spinning in the same spots."

Don't Cross-Contaminate Arena Footing

An indoor arena holds specialized footing, kept pristine for riders—while an outdoor arena deals with leaves, grass, weeds, and wind-blown debris. But if you don't take care of how you maintain that indoor arena, your drag equipment could track in unwanted contaminants, which will negatively affect the footing.

"The key with indoor arenas, is if you can keep one tractor to use just for the arena, that is best," Danny Austin says. "If you are only using one tractor, and it has to do other ranch duties, have a covered zone with a concrete floor where the drag and tractor are stored and cleaned."

The analogy is that driving an outdoor tractor indoors is like wearing muddy boots from outside and walking around your house. The solution to this problem is a "mud room" where you can remove and clean your shoes. The same principle applies to your arena maintenance equipment.

"I see it happen all the time: people spend $200,000 on a brand-new riding surface, but they're taking their tractor out in the gravel and bringing rocks into the arena," Austin says. "If you want to maintain a surface and keep it to that premium level, you need to have a covered place to pull your tractor and drag equipment into and out of."

Maintaining Arenas for Specific Disciplines

Dressage

"With the drags we're going an inch and a half deep for dressage," Attwood says. "For dressage, you're trying to create a surface that has a little bit of life to it, and it's solid and compact."

For an event, dressage is the first of the three phases, and the same arena may be used for stadium jumping later in the competition. An arena prepped for dressage tends to have a couple of percentage points less moisture than jumping, Attwood says. He also drags a bit deeper.

Jumping

Attwood adds more moisture to arena surfaces to prepare it for jumping. The footing should be firm.

"Having that good, solid surface that is more grippy helps the horse get purchase to make the jump," Attwood says. "It allows them to make faster turns."

7.6 Proper moisture in footing in an arena used for jumping adds grip so the horse can get purchase as he approaches and clears the obstacle.

Arena Grooming and Maintenance | 139

For jumping, Attwood smooths the surface and removes hoofprints, while compressing the footing with the drag's rollers.

"You have these forces working to keep the footing nice and tight," Attwood says.

Western and English All-Around

When you measure the moisture content (see p. 106) of an arena for all-around riding, like Western pleasure and English flat classes, you're looking at just a small amount of moisture.

7.7 Western and English all-around events, such as pleasure classes, need less moisture content than a performance horse class. The footing should be smooth and relatively shallow.

Kiser also goes by touch and feel, having maintained ground for major stock horse events for decades.

"You want it just to where it isn't dusty, that's about as much moisture as you want," Kiser says. "If you get much wetter than that, the dirt will stick in feet and pack together. So you want to keep it as dry as you can."

7.8 *Vary the spots where you spin or stop in your reining arena to avoid carving holes into the footing.*

The surface layer should be no more than 2 inches deep, and it should be pretty sandy to avoid too much compaction. Kiser says it should be dragged with a thorough pass across the arena, following one of the patterns illustrated previously (see p. 130).

Snodgress says the footing for all-around events should showcase the horse's quality of movement, so a shallow and slightly compacted surface is ideal. But you don't want it packed down too hard. He aims for the correct amount of sand and clay to achieve the right properties for these events.

Reining

Reining footing needs to maintain its form to allow horses to circle at speed without slipping. You want your footing to be 2¾-inches deep on top of a firm, level base. If your footing is mostly sand, versus more of a sand/silt/clay mixture, Kiser says you'll want it to be 3 inches deep to give the horse enough push and resistance to hold in maneuvers. As mentioned in chapter 5 (p. 110), reining arenas work best at around 5 to 6 percent moisture, Kiser goes on. Sometimes a reining pen will need to be worked several times with the drag before it is ready to be used. If you have it, using a laser level will help ensure your footing is even across the arena.

Snodgress says once you have your base established, avoid using rippers or discs to disturb it. The top layer should be a lighter and fluffier sand with some give to it to aid in stops, yet enough moisture to prevent slipping on circles.

Cow Horse

Footing for cow horse events should be similar to reining—after all, the event consists of a reining pattern and one-on-one cow work—but Kiser suggests deepening the top layer to 3 inches, although you do want to watch that you don't get the footing too deep.

"Too deep footing will really affect their turnarounds [spins]," Kiser says.

For cow horse, you want more moisture content to firm up the ground. Kiser aims for 6 to 7 percent moisture content. Sliding stops will not be as flashy, but going down the fence and circling up the cow will be much safer.

"The reason we go to more moisture is it gives a little more hold when they're under a lot of stress," Kiser says. "It makes it a little bit safer. Their stops would be a little tougher, but it's really to help when they're chasing the cow."

Cutting

Cutting sand does not need to be super deep, contrary to popular opinion, Kiser says. He says the deepest he's made the dirt at major National Cutting Horse Association events such as the NCHA Futurity, Derby and Super Stakes—all held at the Coliseum at Will Rogers Memorial Center in Fort Worth, Texas—is 4 inches. And it's usually 3½ to 3¾ inches deep.

"In the practice pen, it's only 3 inches," Kiser says. "That's all they want, so that they don't wear their horses out."

In some arenas specifically designed for cutting, Kiser has seen the sand at 5 and 6 inches deep, but he says they're using washed concrete sand, which offers more grip, "but you can't hardly walk across that sand."

Moisture content for a primarily sand cutting arena should be maintained at around 7 percent, Kiser says, 8 percent at the most.

"If it looks like those horses are sliding just a little bit too far as they're going back and forth with a cow, the next time you drag, give it another shot of water," Kiser recommends.

7.9 *The sand in a cutting arena does not need to be kept excessively deep, as some believe. Maintain moisture content around 7 percent.*

The drag pattern for a cutting class is basically going in circles.

"About all you can do is change your direction and try to come across the middle a time or two," Kiser says. "There's not a lot else you can do. That's where I started using the laser during the horse show to keep the footing consistent."

Snodgress says the area of the arena where the cattle stand can get wet and sloppy, requiring the maintenance crew to change up the pattern of dragging to mix wetter dirt with the drier dirt farther away from the herd. He also says for an arena dedicated to cutting, the footing may need to be replaced more frequently because of the amount of urine and manure a herd of cattle produces.

"Your drag can get the footing perfect for where the cutting and turnback people are, but where the cattle stand, it tends to pack down and get really hard," Snodgress says. "So you may drag the arena and you're moving dirt around to fill in holes and level other spots, but when you get to that hard spot, your drag may raise up because the tractor tires aren't sinking into the dirt as much, which dumps a lot of the dirt on top of it. If you keep doing that, it's going to build up."

Barrel Racing

When preparing your arena for barrel racing, it's not quite as deep as cutting and will have a higher moisture level than other events, Snodgress suggests. He says barrel ground may have more clay, because it needs to hold together so horses don't slip around the turns. Arena crews drag frequently at barrel races—sometimes between every three to five runs. The challenge is replacing the footing in the holes created by horses going around the barrels.

"You want to hit the high spot of the dirt from the backside, take it back into the hole, and drag it away from the holes," Snodgress says. "It's important to change directions every once in a while to make sure you don't start getting dips. We level everything so that when it rains, you don't have a hole that fills up with water."

You'll want to go into a barrel arena and drag going to the left one time, then go in the next and circle to the right, says Snodgress.

Similar to moving reining maneuver practice around an arena, Kiser recommends moving your barrels to slightly different areas periodically to avoid digging holes in the ground from repeated turns in the same spots (see more about maintaining arenas used for barrels on p. 148).

7.10 For barrel racing, Leland Smith changes direction every time he drags to make sure he's bringing dirt back into the holes around the barrels.

Halter

When creating footing for halter and showmanship classes, Austin says the criteria has to be a surface humans can comfortably walk on without tripping. Staff at an equine facility that fits and conditions halter horses will often lead horses from a golf cart for exercise, so the ground needs to be somewhat shallow to allow for easy travel.

"We have a base, but we have a much shallower footing," Austin says. "It's mainly to keep that horse where they've got good footfall support to where they're not feeling like they're on ice."

The footing should be no more than 1½-inch deep on top of a firmer, compacted layer of the same material—or a clay or limestone base, Kiser says. To achieve this depth, his team sets the drag to smooth the ground similar to sealing it off before a rain shower.

"We're just going over the ground and run over it a few times to get it firmed up," he explains.

Your moisture content for halter should be 3 to 4 percent, which is just enough to control dust.

CASE STUDY

KEEP IT RIGHT FOR THE COWBOYS

Randy Spraggins has handled the footing for many major rodeos, including the Wrangler National Finals Rodeo (WNFR). The rodeos he maintains ground for include multiple events back-to-back: timed events such as team roping, tie-down roping, and steer wrestling; barrel racing, and roughstock events, including bull riding, bareback, and saddle bronc riding. It's a challenge to prepare ground in a way that is safe and satisfactory for all competitors, Spraggins says.

"To make the ground work for everybody in rodeo is a big bite to chew off," Spraggins says. "But what I've learned is, if you make the ground good for the barrel racers, it's pretty much good for everybody."

One of the biggest challenges Spraggins encounters is the wide variety of dirt he works with because he's doing dirt installations and maintenance in arenas across the country—indoor and outdoor. Some arenas he has to blend the soil already there. Others he's building the arena from a concrete pad where basketball games—or even ice hockey matches—were held just prior to the event.

"Every week is a challenge—you have different people, different equipment, different weather, different ground, and you try to make it work week in and week out," Spraggins says.

Steer wrestlers come off the horse, hit the ground, and as they're wrestling the cow to the ground, they need to be able to slide on their feet without breaking bones. Tie-down ropers come off the horse, hit the ground, and run on foot to the calf.

"For these cowboys, when they hit the ground, their footwork is just as important as the horses', and they need to have a good impact and good feel for the ground," Spraggins says.

For roughstock events (bronc and bull riding), the horses and the bulls are also looking for stable footing.

"If they're comfortable, and it feels good, they buck harder," Spraggins says. "I've been doing dirt

7.11 Rodeo footing needs to be groomed in a way that offers support for fast turns in barrel racing and cushioning for rough stock riders, and still allow cowboys on foot to run easily for tie-down roping.

for bull riding for almost 40 years, but to get them to come to their full potential is if the bull feels good, he's going to work harder. That goes for all the animals."

The barrel racers for the WNFR bring their horses into the pen to practice and let their horses get used to the arena so they can charge into the pen during their runs in the rodeo. "We try to maintain that footing for all 10 days, and we try to make it consistent as well as safe," Spraggins says. "We try to find the happy spot and then stay there."

Throughout the WNFR's 10 days of rodeo performances, Spraggins says the maintenance crew may tweak small things after the rodeo each night to get the dirt prepared. Sometimes they work the ground a little deeper, other times they add more water. The goal is to give all of the competitors clean runs, with no issues on the dirt.

If the footing doesn't have the right amount of moisture, it can get what Spraggins refers to as a "hard pan" where the top layer is good, but the layer below it is hard and slick. This is preferred in an arena where riders are doing reining, but it can cause rodeo competitors to slip or stumble.

"The horse is just looking to drive, and if he doesn't have anything to push off of, you need to have ground where he can get down through a couple of layers," Spraggins says. "You need the dirt to move, but then stop moving so he can push off of it."

Spraggins will test the footing at the events he does, particularly big rodeos like the NFR and The American. He works with a soil lab to profile the dirt.

"When I started doing this years ago, I took 50 samples of what I considered really good dirt around the country, and we looked at the composition and found the parts of them that were consistent," Spraggins explains. "So that gives us a target value we try to get to."

If the soil test shows there's too much sand in the mixture, he'll add some clay, or vice versa—too much clay, he'll add sand. He also looks at the particle size.

"There are certain sand blends that we like to combine with different sizes of materials to get us where we want to be," Spraggins says. "We have amendments where we can take questionable ground and amend it a little bit, turn it the way we want, and we've been pretty successful with that. It all starts in the lab. You need to know what your ground is."

Once you get the arena footing blend, Spraggins says the tools you're using such as your tractor and drag are key. And the moisture levels are extremely important.

Traveling around the country to manage the footing at different rodeos, Spraggins brings Kiser implements with him to some events. Others he works with the local arena crew and their equipment. All with the goal of making the footing be the best it can be for that event.

Some events Spraggins is starting from scratch, moving the dirt onto a bare floor, preparing it for the rodeo, maintaining it throughout the event and then removing the dirt at the end of the rodeo. One such event is the All In Race in Las Vegas—a major barrel race. There, he uses a custom blend manufactured material.

"We pre-process it with water until we feel it's close to what we want before we haul it into the building, and we keep it that way by watering. We watch the moisture content, because your outside temperatures and humidity levels make a difference, even for an indoor arena."

Spraggins says he monitors the footing visually and by feeling it, because after decades of working with rodeo ground, he knows what it should look and feel like. But he has started to use some measuring instruments at the WNFR.

"We have a ground penetrating device that reads the moisture level, and we can see when it changes a percentage or two, so we know when we need to add a little more water or back off a little bit."

He has found if his crew is struggling to maintain a consistent moisture level—say in an arid location like Vegas—watering at night and working the ground the next day works best.

For an outdoor rodeo, Spraggins is battling Mother Nature—100-plus degree temperatures influence how much water he needs to apply. Sometimes he'll add more water than what would make the footing ideal in anticipation of it drying out in the heat.

For an indoor, the conditions are still affected by weather. On a hot day he'll work with the HVAC company serving the facility to manage the amount of air flowing—too much air and the footing will dry out during the rodeo, causing inconsistencies and other issues.

"If the air is on too high, the effects on the facility are noticeable—the ground gets too dry and dust starts getting everywhere," Spraggins says. "And a lot of the facilities we work in are professional sports facilities for NBA, NHL, and they're very particular about the cleanliness of their facility after the event is over. We try to control things on our end with our water application and how we work the ground."

Cheyenne Frontier Days in Cheyenne, Wyoming, famously has rainstorms that hit during the July rodeo. The arena has been built to drain exceptionally well, says Spraggins.

"It could be a sloppy mess on top, but there's still good footing down below because it evacuates the water really well."

Sometimes heavy rain is too great of an obstacle, and Spraggins will work with the rodeo management to make a decision to postpone events such as barrel racing till the following day, when conditions are safer. He says he can do a lot of things to help recover ground, but at the end of the day, you also depend on elements like a sunny day, warm temperatures, and a breeze to dry out footing.

"Daily conditions can change, you have to roll with the punches, and there's no cookie cutter way to care for the ground each day," he admits. "Each event is specific, and when Mother Nature comes into play, this sets the tone and rules the roost."

CHAPTER 8

REPAIRING AND ASSESSING YOUR ARENA

The lifespan of an average equestrian arena ranges anywhere from 3 to 20 years, depending on the materials in the footing, fencing, and any cover or building, and how it is used and maintained. Every arena will at some point require repair, but with careful maintenance, you can extend its life. This chapter will discuss signs your arena has problems, primarily with the footing and base, that need to be addressed, as well as provide a review of the elements that should be regularly assessed as to whether they are meeting your standards for safe riding and training.

Problems with Footing

Nick Attwood says a lot of problems with classic—sand/silt/clay—footing, such as being too firm or too deep, can be addressed by adding the right sand to the mixture.

"Sometimes when it's too deep, it's because the sand particles are too large and smooth—like beach sand—and it doesn't bind together," he explains. "The way to make it bind is to add a finer sand to the footing."

The amount you add depends on your situation, but adding 20 to 30 percent of the total footing volume with a finer sand is something Attwood has done.

"Let's say we have a 100- by 200-foot arena, and it has about 300 tons of footing," Attwood relays. "We might take 50 or 60 tons of very fine sand, blend it in and mix it up, and re-lay it, and that will 'tighten' the footing up."

Another way to tighten up loose footing is by adding textiles. Attwood says to mix the fiber with the footing you already have, your best bet is to remove

> **EXPERT TIP**
>
> Before making any drastic moves to repair your footing, always consider whether you have the right moisture content in your arena (see chapter 5—p. 106).
>
> "Adding more moisture often will help—getting the correct amount of moisture can address loose footing," Nick Attwood says.

8.1 *The lifespan of an arena depends on what your ground is made of and how you use and care for it. Proper maintenance is the key to a safe riding, training, or competition space.*

all the current footing, mix it with fiber, and then re-lay it.

"If you only have a couple of inches of sand, and you start to add textiles to it [directly], the way the textiles interact with the sand and knit it all together will make it very difficult to drag. You need to pull the footing off the base, unless you have at least 4 inches of sand."

Footing that is too firm can be amended with a coarser sand. A footing that is too firm may have a high clay content, Attwood says. When you want to make the footing more suitable for English events, consider adding coarse sand in a similar 20 to 30 percent ratio.

"That's a good place to get started, and blend the two sands together," Attwood says. "The coarse sand will prevent it from compacting down into such a hard surface."

This is also a situation where adding rubber to your footing can help improve it.

When Sand "Wears Out"

Even footing that seems as durable as sand or clay can wear out. Bob Kiser says this is due to a couple of factors: the amount of force a horse's hooves exert as they hit the ground, and the steel of a drag as a tractor pulls it through the footing.

"Most sand is not extremely hard," Kiser says. "When you buy river sand, it's just a soft sand. You can take a grain of it, hit it with a hammer, and it'll break. It'll get finer and finer. Next thing you know, you've got silt instead of sand."

When you have sand footing, there's an easy way to tell when it has started to break down, Kiser says. When you water your arena or experience rainfall, if the water stays on top of the footing for hours instead of soaking in and drying within a day or two, it may have higher levels of silt and organic matter that are slowing down the process of infiltration.

Nick Attwood says when sand has broken down into finer particles, it'll bind the footing together and

EXPERT TIP

Danny Austin suggests taking a sample of your footing when you first put it in your arena—even place it in a plastic bag—to compare to your footing down the road. "A year or two later, take another sample and compare what you've got," he says. "You can gauge how your footing is doing that way. It sneaks up on people. The arena will be great, they're so happy with it, and then it's like a light switch. But actually your arena has been changing the whole time, you just don't notice the changes because you're riding on the same arena every day."

the result is firmer footing. You'll notice because it can be difficult to drag.

Revitalizing Sand Footing

There are two ways to fix footing when the sand has broken down.

"There's the cheap way, and the expensive way," Kiser says. "The cheap way is to add more sand, which will get you by for a year before you need to add more sand. The other way is to take it all out and start over."

Eventually sand may get beyond repair and need to be completely replaced, but many arenas do well with just adding sand, Kiser says. There is a process to doing it correctly, though. You need to be sure you are using the right type of sand—test the composition to assure it is suitable for your arena.

Problems with the Base

When it's necessary, Kiser will excavate all the footing down to the sub base, and start over. One arena he worked on recently was full of holes and dangerous for riding and training horses. On this project, he took the top sand off the arena, watered the base, ripped it up, reprocessed it, and laid it back down, compacted it, and put new sand back on top.

Austin often sees holes in areas where horses have been longed, or where they've been tied up along the rail. A common method folks use to try to repair them is to pull a little bit of the sand back from that area, throw on similar base material, and cover it back up.

"The hole pops right back out in a week," Austin says. "Any base repair, if you're going to do anything on your own, you have to dig *past* the damage zone into a good section to make repairs. It's like replacing a pothole in a road."

When your arena has standing water after it rains, Austin says take note of the puddle size. Then take a shovel, dig down to your base, and see if there is a dip in the base in that area. Take a box level or a straight edge, put it across the base and see if there's a deviation or a low spot. That way you can schedule a base repair for that area.

"You want to see why the water is standing there. Is it because it's not being evenly dragged and there's an inconsistent amount of footing?" he says. "Or is there some base damage?"

Austin cautions about doing a repair on your base yourself: "You could turn a small problem into a major issue—conservative is always better. Don't get in over your head because it's hard to go backward."

If you've used an unsuitable material for the base material that doesn't pack hard enough, it can fall

REPAIRING DRAINAGE ISSUES

If your arena is not draining correctly, your base could have a low spot that collects water. Attwood says you can scrape back the footing and install a French drain into the base with a pipe that exits the arena, giving the water somewhere to go.

"A French drain in an arena can take on all kinds of different looks," he explains. "You dig a trench, put a piece of perforated pipe at the bottom—which exits the arena through a solid pipe—cover it with drain rock, put fabric over the top, followed by putting the top footing back in place."

A product called Easy Flow is a 3-inch corrugated, perforated pipe surrounded by material similar to packing peanuts, about an inch in size, held in place by a fabric sac.

"You can buy Easy Flow sections, peel back your footing in your arena, dig a trench to put down the perforated Easy Flow pipe, and cover it up about 2 or 3 inches below the level of the base," Attwood says. "You'll have a gap that gets filled up with footing, and typically that will help drain the arena as well."

apart, Attwood warns. The best way he has found to fix a disintegrating base is to excavate all the footing and determine the state of the base.

"You've got to make a decision about what you're going to do with the material underneath," Attwood says. "Often it's just easier to 'put a cap on it' with the right material, 2 or 3 inches."

Sometimes you may have an arena that was built with the wrong materials. For example, if the base has gravel made with rocks that are too large, they will invariably create holes when one comes loose.

"When your base material starts to fall apart in certain areas, then you can get stones in your footing," Attwood says. "The only way to fix that is to scrape all the footing off, put a 'cap' on top of the base material—that is around 2 to 3 inches of base material that is more suitable. Otherwise the stones will keep coming up."

Whenever your arena is too deep, or inconsistent, Austin says the likely problem is often the arena was not built correctly to begin with.

"If the elevations aren't squared, or the percentage of the slope is not accurate, the footing won't be consistent," he explains. "In those cases, the fence is already built, and we have to break the bad news that

> **EXPERT TIP**
>
> You can use a rock picker to remove rocks from your arena. Bob Kiser says the best ones are the kind used as beach cleaners.

there's really no way to get the arena perfect until we tear down the entire fence. It's sometimes really tough to actually repair an arena properly without starting completely over."

WHEN DO YOU NEED TO REPAIR YOUR FOOTING OR BASE?

The bad news is, if you think you may have an issue with your footing, you probably have a bigger problem than you realize, Austin says. It is worth your time to hire a consultant or a competent arena specialist (see p. 90) to help you evaluate the state of your arena and suggest repairs.

If you come in and just add sand without looking into it, you're just covering up the issue," he warns. "Usually the issues start at the bottom and show their ugly head at the top."

If your arena is holding water, get on top of the issue as soon as possible. Don't assume it'll dissipate without causing damage.

"If you have an outdoor arena and you see water standing, it's going to weaken the base, it's going to further deteriorate and wreck that arena," Austin says. "When you see little issues rise up, try to catch them in a hurry and address them. It's a lot easier to take care of them when it's a small issue rather than a big issue."

Getting Arena Feedback

If you get feedback from riders using your arena that your footing is "bad," you'll need to investigate why.

"If someone tells me the ground is bad, I ask, 'What was bad about it?'" Austin says. "Most people can't tell you, but good trainers will know exactly what feels wrong. Maybe they're out there running their fast circles and it feels like the horse isn't underneath them."

Sometimes, bad ground is missing something. It could be needing a bit of silt and clay. It might have sand that's too pure or too coarse that makes the footing feel slippery. Or it could be not enough moisture, or too much moisture, or a bad ratio between materials.

Sometimes bad ground has simply been dragged at the wrong depth to make it too deep. This can be corrected with drag depth adjustments, grooming, and water.

"You can take the poorest ground in the world and make it better if you know what you're doing with it," Austin says. "Reach out to somebody and get them to help you, get it figured out."

Other Common Arena Issues

Burrowing Animals

Depending on where you live, you may encounter burrowing animals, such as moles or prairie dogs. They can dig into your arena and wreak havoc on the footing. If you notice these pesky animals making a home in your arena, you'll need to take action.

Attwood once built an indoor arena, and animals tunneled under the building.

"The arena completely collapsed, and the owners had no idea it was about to happen," he says. "You may have to dig a trench, and put up a barrier to stop them digging and coming under the arena. You have to stop the animals from being able to burrow in underneath, and then you've got to fix the base before you put [the footing] all back."

Uneven Footing

If your base is perfectly flat, and you have 3 or 4 inches of footing, over time, the way you drag the arena can affect the level. When you repeat your drag pattern, you'll end up with areas which are a little deeper and areas a little shallower.

"The tractor can lean a little bit into the corners, and the drag will take a little bit of the footing," Attwood says. "And then as you're coming around the short side, and then going in a straight line, the drag can drop a little bit of footing. It's minuscule, every time. But after six months of going round and round, you've moved footing from the corners and you've put it in the center of the short sides."

This is a common issue, and you might not observe it because it happens so gradually. But eventually, you'll notice you don't have enough footing in the corners. This is difficult to prevent, Attwood admits.

The easy and cheap way to fix it? Take a shovel and walk around to see where the high spots are of the material. When you find them, scoop them up and throw the sand back in the shallower spots.

"It doesn't take much work to rake it and shovel from the high spots into the low spots, maybe two or three hours," Attwood says.

An alternate (and more expensive) method is to get your arena laser-graded so that it's perfectly level and even across the space.

Dripping Sprinkler Heads

This may be a surprising issue, but if you have an overhead sprinkler, it could be dripping water onto your arena, and that can start to erode your base underneath your footing.

"Regularly maintain your sprinklers, and if you

notice any that aren't working properly, replace them," Attwood says.

Keeping an eye out for problems like these, and considering the assessment points that follow, will allow you to be proactive in handling issues with your arena. Paired with good maintenance, you'll be on your way to having a safe and consistent riding and training space ideal for your horses and your activities.

Arena Assessment

Maintaining an arena is a daunting task. The overarching goal is safe, consistent footing for your horse, suited to your particular discipline. Every time your horse steps out into your arena, you want it to be the best footing possible.

So what does good footing look like? How can you tell if your footing needs to be adjusted, modified, or repaired? Walk through this checklist, and you'll have a good idea of where to begin.

Start with Unmaintained Footing

When you're digging for info about the status of your arena, don't drag before you start your investigation.

ARENA REPAIR EVALUATION

Danny Austin goes through several steps to evaluate a problematic arena and determine which issues may need to be repaired:

1. Check the elevations. Find out what grade your base is, and make sure it's the level you need for your particular location.

2. Check the compaction of the base. Did you use the right material when building the pad?

3. Overhaul your drag techniques. Do you have the right equipment? Are you dragging in a way that tears up your base, or creates footing that is too deep or too shallow for your needs?

4. Consider moisture. Are you applying the right amount of water to your footing, at the right times, often enough?

Nick Attwood says he's had clients ask him to help them repair their footing, but when he arrives, the arena looks good.

"If you drag it just before we get there, we can't see anything—there are no clues," Attwood says. "A dragged arena looks amazing, but it can cover up a whole series of problems."

Walk and Observe

Instead, start by walking around on top of the footing and observing the hoofprints. You can also gain information by watching horses perform on the footing.

"Many riders can feel a lot when they're riding," Attwood says. "They can give you feedback about what is happening beneath their horse's feet. The horse can tell you if the footing is working or not."

Don't survey your footing from the seat of your tractor, Austin agrees. Walk your arena at least once a week. When you have an area that feels inconsistent when you're walking or riding on it, there is probably something wrong and you should get it checked.

"Check your depth on your arena," he says. "If you have a base and a footing type of arena with two components, check for any contamination of the base coming up in to the footing. Check all your corners, edges, center."

"You can use a shovel or a probe and check your depth," Austin says. "Make sure you're staying consistent, and if it starts to get out of whack, maintenance is the key."

Pay Attention While Dragging

While dragging, look for potential issues. On an outdoor arena, check your perimeter and make sure sand isn't getting up over the rail. Make sure the drainage is still in place. Is grass growing in the corners? Is sand pulled down from the edges so rain can sheet off the arena?

"I've seen people just go in and drag and keep on going," Austin says. "They're scraping up the base just because they're not paying attention."

EXPERT TIP

When you have grass in your arena, Danny Austin says you need to pull it by hand—do not drag it out across the rest of the arena!

Survey the Arena

Measure:

- How level the base is.
- How much footing you have.
- How evenly the footing is distributed.

To measure these elements, Nick Attwood uses a laser.

"It's like a lighthouse," Attwood says. "It sends out a [horizontal] beam of light. In its simplest form, that beam of light is perfectly flat to the surface of the earth. You're shooting out a reference point that is going around in circles. A device the size of a smart phone has a detector on it that can detect the light."

This device can identify differences in height in inches or centimeters. Grid off the arena, and walk across the spaces, taking a measurement every 20 feet along the length and width.

"You'll have five or six measurements going across, and you'll build a picture," Attwood says.

Measure the Base

When you already have footing in your arena, you will need to scrape away your footing to expose the base to gather information about its degree of levelness.

"Once that is finished, you'll have a picture of your base," Attwood says. "If it's outdoors, you'll be able to see how much of a slope you have, and if it's close to what it should be."

As mentioned in chapter 4 (see p. 78), your base needs to slope in a flat plane down the longer side. What you do not want in any arena are "waves" of elevation throughout. Even a change in elevation of 1 inch can significantly affect the quality of your arena. This contributes to drainage issues, inconsistent footing, and more.

"If you want a top-quality arena, every layer needs to be a perfect plane, from the base to the top," Attwood says. "If you have a perfect flat plane with your base, then you can laser grade the footing on top and make it consistent. Consistency of the grade is key to building or improving an arena."

Measure the Footing

You can gather information about your footing, when your arena has the surface layers installed.

"As you walk around and on those same points as you did on the base, you can take the same measurements with the [top] footing, and do simple arithmetic," Attwood says. "The footing should be 3 or 4 inches, or whatever depth you need, above the base."

You'll be able to calculate the amount of actual footing with that information, and an average depth.

Knowing if your footing is consistent across the arena is extremely important. If you don't have enough footing in some areas, you may actually have too much footing in other areas.

"You can go around the arena with the lasers and measure the footing, and you can see where you need to move footing to make the whole arena the

> **EXPERT TIP**
>
> Bob Kiser explains that footing is measured in cubic yards. The formula for determining cubic yards per square feet of arena (how much footing you need) looks like this example:
>
> A 70-foot by 200-foot arena is 14,000 square feet.
>
> Divide 14,000 by 27 (3 feet in a yard, and 3 yards cubed), which is 518.5.
>
> Divide 518.5 by 12 (inches in a foot), which is 43.2 cubic yards.
>
> You would then multiply that times every inch of footing you desire (or example, 3 inches) to find out how much footing you need to cover a 70-foot by 200-foot arena.

same depth," Attwood says. "That's why the survey is so important. You're using the power of numbers, instead of basically just guessing. I like to try to keep all guessing out of working on arenas."

Signs Your Footing Is Too Deep

- Hoofprints leave deep holes.
- Hoofprints leave no holes at all (fill back in) because it's too loose and deep.
- Footing is too hard with no indentations.

It's extremely helpful to know how many inches of footing you have. When you feel like your footing is too deep, you can calculate how much footing you need to remove. Once you know how many cubic yards of footing you have, your footing supplier can calculate that number of tons.

Signs Your Footing Is Too Shallow

- Too firm.
- Horses or drag are hitting the base.

When you feel like your footing is not deep enough, you can calculate how many more inches deep you need, and then translate that number into the amount of footing you need to add (see sidebar for the formula).

Check Sand Gradations

Look at the composition of the footing materials. Perhaps your footing packs together too much and water ponds on top instead of draining easily. This could be a result of the blend having too much silt because the sand has broken down from age or use.

Attwood says evaluating the sand gradation is fairly

straightforward: take a sample and send to a lab that does sand gradations, and sand/silt/clay analysis. If you've purchased a manufactured footing, you may be able to send your footing to the company that made it for a sand analysis.

"If you've added textiles to your footing, let's say five years ago, you can find out what you've got left," Attwood says. "It's very simple to separate the sand and the textiles."

Doing a sand gradation test will give you concrete numbers to work from. You can then work with an arena consultant to add materials as needed to improve your footing.

"The gradation of the sand in combination with working out the weight of it and if there's an additive alongside the sand, the companies that sell these additives know what the ratio should be," Attwood emphasizes.

Check Moisture Content

Ask yourself:

- Is your method of adding water to your arena working?
- Do you have even coverage of moisture in your arena?
- Is your arena too wet or too dry?

Refer to chapter 5 (p. 106) for more information about how to measure and manage the moisture in your arena. You can evaluate how much moisture you have in your arena using a moisture meter. This is helpful in a couple of ways.

"If you have an arena that has a sprinkler system, you can run the sprinkler, drag your arena, and then go around and measure the moisture content," Attwood says. "You might find that it's pretty evenly distributed, or you might find it's not, and half the sprinklers aren't putting out as much water—or maybe some aren't delivering any water."

When you find your sprinklers aren't delivering consistent moisture, you'll want to adjust or repair the malfunctioning sprinkler heads. Check the settings on your control box. You may need to adjust how long different zones are watered.

Check Over Maintenance Equipment

Ask yourself:

- Do you have the right equipment for your arena?
- Is your drag hooked up correctly?
- Are your settings on your drag correct for the task?
- Does your drag work as designed?
- Is your tractor powerful enough to adequately pull your implement?
- Are your tires aired up to the same amount of air pressure?

Even if you have the right drag, you need to make sure you have attached it to your tractor correctly and that the drag is perfectly level. And the equipment must be set to the desired settings to do the job. Look over your drag and make sure you have no broken or missing teeth, the wheels and bearings are greased, and all pieces are working.

Your tractor needs to be set in four-wheel drive to work the arena, Attwood says. Your tires need to be aired up to the exact same level.

"If the tires are not at the same amount of air pressure, it'll make dragging your arena a mess because the tractor will be leaning," Attwood says. "If you go around a corner and you have a flat on one tire, the tractor will lean even more. You're just making it harder for yourself."

Evaluate Your Drag Patterns

- Are you dragging at the right speed?
- Are you varying your pattern?
- Are you paying close attention to how you're dragging?

I covered drag patterns in detail in chapter 7 (p. 129), but no matter what event you're dragging for, or the type of footing you have, you need to make sure you are not dragging the same direction every time. Don't do the same pattern—start by going right one time and left the next. Switch it up to keep the footing more even across the arena.

Maintaining your arena, using good quality materials, ensuring it is suitable to the space and the desired type of riding, are all important steps in providing your horses with safe, correct footing. With help from the information provided here, I hope you will have many years of riding in the best arena possible.

CHAPTER 9

RACETRACKS

Racetracks are the stage on which horses become legends. There is no more visible equine sport in the world than horse racing—for good and bad. To manipulate such a large outdoor space into footing that is consistent, safe, and encourages a horse's best performance is a huge task. But every day, racetrack managers around the world do just that.

In this chapter, I'll discuss how racetrack construction, footing, and maintenance differs from what we do with arenas. I'll include helpful info for those who are curious about racetracks, who own or train on a racetrack, or who just want to be more knowledgeable about footing conditions before betting on a race.

The Goal for Track Surfaces

Mick Peterson, Ph.D., is the director of the University of Kentucky's Racetrack Safety Program and the executive director of the Racing Services Testing Laboratory. He has been instrumental in developing research-backed protocols for building and maintaining tracks around the United States.

"I half-jokingly, but in all seriousness, tell people that if we are successful, the superintendents at the racetracks view their job as minimizing the development of musculoskeletal disease in the horse," Peterson says. "We are not only protecting the horse, we're protecting the rider. We are protecting the horse and the rider by keeping the horse upright and avoiding catastrophic injuries or career-ending injuries."

Former Lone Star Park track superintendent and track surface consultant George McDermott says the track superintendent's main job is ensuring the safety of the horse and rider. That involves listening to feedback from trainers, riders, and veterinarians.

"We just want to understand how to get those horses across the track safely, which protects the lives of all of the riders," McDermott says. "You're protecting the rider by making it safe for the horse to go across the track."

9.1 The primary goal of racetrack supervisors and their maintenance crews is to get horses and jockeys around the track safely.

The Science of Strides

Unlike arenas, racetracks are built and maintained for one sport, where horses gallop straight and make left-handed turns around the track. Peterson has done extensive research on the biomechanics of equine movement. Here he explains the phases of a horse's stride.

"The horse is going 35, 40 miles an hour," he says. "The hoof is stopped a portion of the time, and then it flies through the air and catches up with the horse. Then it stops."

Primary Impact: When the horse puts the hoof mass against the surface of the track.

Secondary Impact: When the weight of the horse is transferred onto the leg of the horse. "The weight of the horse dynamically loads the hoof," Peterson says. "That's about two and a half times the body weight on the load of the foot because you've got the mass of the body moving down onto the hoof."

Stance Phase: The body of the horse is moving forward over the hoof.

Propulsion: Breakover, where the toes penetrate down into the surface of the track and propels the horse forward.

Swing Phase: The hoof is in the air. "The horse is going 35 miles per hour at that point, but the hoof has to go up to 70 miles an hour, because otherwise it gets left behind because it was stopped part of the time," Peterson explains.

Peterson says racetracks can be designed around the phases of a horse's gallop. "When the racetrack is functioning properly, that initial impact is softened by the cushioning of the top, the harrowed top surface. That harrowed top surface is there to decelerate the hoof smoothly as it hits. The harrow goes around after every race before you race on it again."

The hoof lands vertically at 60 miles per hour, going through the cushion. "The whole purpose of the loose upper cushion is to decelerate the hoof," Peterson says. "But then you need to be able to support it. So the hoof is both slowing down at that point, but going quickly into the secondary impact, so you have to support the hoof as it's coming down."

Underneath the fluffy top surface is a hard pan layer that supports the hoof.

"The real challenge for the racetrack is during that

9.2 Being located very close to the Pacific Ocean means Del Mar Racetrack encounters variables such as humidity, wind, and sun.

secondary impact," Peterson goes on. "A little bit of slide is good because you're not going to load the bones as rapidly. And the speed at which the bones are loaded is what stimulates bone remodeling. And while some bone remodeling is needed, excess is also a problem."

Peterson says you want some bone remodeling—a natural process of the bone replacing itself—but not too much because it can result in musculoskeletal diseases.

"The real challenge is you want the hoof to slide a little bit, but then you want the footing to support it, when the horse begins to go into the propulsive stage and accelerates the horse forward," Peterson says. "You have to have a surface underneath this loose cushion that is hard enough to support the horse, but soft enough to allow the toe to get a bit of a grip on it so the horse can propel itself forward."

Racetrack Construction

A racetrack needs to be built with the accuracy of a soccer field, but they look more like building a road, Peterson says.

"You're building something 80 feet wide and a mile long," he explains. "That's a decent medium-size road."

Whether you're building a turf, synthetic, or dirt

track, the foundation is similar to a road base on a rural road, or a harness track.

"Regional differences in racetracks are primarily driven by two things: one, the lack of water in the Southwest, which means that the design historically developed for completely different reasons in a different design," Peterson says. "In the Northeast, it's absolutely critical that they have the design they have because when they race in the winter, they have to have a shallow sand track."

A shallow sand track allows the horses to race in the evenings in the winter and keeps the track from freezing for longer. Once the track does begin to freeze, the ice forms in small balls, not chunks.

"I call it a 'four-phase track,'" Peterson says. "It's got air, water, ice, and sand, with little ice crystals in it. That's how they race in the winter in the Northeast."

McDermott says racetracks have several styles. "There is 'East Coast style,' which is 'short cushion' racetracks. In other words, the depth of the material on the surface of the racetrack might be 3½ inches."

'West Coast style' has closer to 9 to 12 inches of material. Louisiana tracks have perhaps 5 to 6 inches, he says. No matter the location, track superintendents have to be knowledgeable of how the material used binds together. They also have to keep in mind the regional differences and seasonal climates.

Track Surface Materials

Turf

Turf racing used to be a niche in horse racing, Peterson says. Only about 10 percent of all the starts (in the United States) were on turf, even as recently as 10 to 15 years ago. But it is now gaining in popularity and accounts for over 20 percent of the starts.

"The differences in turf are the turf species," Peterson explains. "*Warm weather turf* is Bermuda. *Cool weather turf* would be Kentucky bluegrass, or rye, or other cool weather grasses. That's a big distinction."

Turf tracks are built differently from those with other surfaces because drainage is even more critical, says Peterson. And depending on the region where a track is located, the track's design could differ. The drainage in a turf track consists of coarse sand underneath the growing medium, combined with an array of drainage pipes. (The soil profile—the sand that is used and the growing medium—can vary.) The drainage not only removes water coming in from the top but in some areas also ensures rising groundwater does not saturate the track.

Jim Pendergest, Director of Racing Surfaces at Keeneland in Lexington, Kentucky, says there are drain tiles below the track, running around the circumference, with outlets to allow the water to escape to the infield. There is coarse sand above the drains, and a finer sand as you get closer to the turf.

No matter the location, just like with a grass arena (see p. 52), the impact of hooves can damage turf. Peterson says mixing fiber into the sand below the grass helps the track recover more quickly.

"By adding some fiber, it adds to the root system and allows it to be beat up pretty hard," he explains. "It's especially important early in the life of a turf racetrack, when you're trying to develop the grass-root system."

Peterson prefers the reinforcement provided by the roots of the grass surface over synthetic fibers.

"Unlike synthetic fibers, the grass grows back. The problem with synthetic fibers, they gradually turn to dust and don't grow back. Whereas you take a root from Bermuda grass and not only is it very strong, but it keeps growing back when it gets damaged."

Synthetic

A racetrack with a synthetic surface is made with rubber or plastic, or sand with a wax coating. Peterson says these days a synthetic track is less likely to have crumb rubber and more likely to have other elastomers or polymers added. This mixture is similar to a synthetic footing used in many arenas in the United Kingdom.

"Synthetic racetracks are safer than dirt tracks, but the upkeep is difficult, and they change with temperature—they've got a number of challenges," Peterson says. "But I think the opportunity there is huge. It's very hopeful."

Some horsemen dislike synthetic track surfaces because the related biomechanics of the horse are different than with natural materials. However, they are actually safer—there are fewer catastrophic injuries on synthetic footing than on dirt or turf.

"I attribute improved safety almost exclusively to the fact that they are less sensitive to moisture content," Peterson says.

In areas with more consistent temperatures, like Golden Gate Fields in northern California, synthetic tracks present fewer difficulties for maintenance. They are also well suited for tracks that race seasonally, like Turfway Park, in Florence, Kentucky, since the range of operating temperatures tends to be lower.

Dirt

About 70 percent of racetracks around the United States are made with natural materials, Peterson says. The composition varies from track to track. And it often varies by region.

"If you take the Southwest, most of the racetracks are not that different from each other," Peterson says.

"The racetracks have a lower clay content than an arena used in a Western discipline but more silt and clay than a typical Eastern racetrack. If you installed those tracks in the Northeast, or you put those tracks in, they would turn into a mud pit as soon as it rained or when the ice thawed in the winter. The spring would just be a disaster. In Southern California or New Mexico, you don't have to worry about it as much. In fact, if it rains, you might just call it quits for a couple days and let everybody enjoy the unusual weather."

Regardless of the location, having the correct moisture content across the track, and equipment to maintain a consistent surface, can go a long way toward improving the safety of a dirt racetrack, he says. "For the last couple of years, the safest major racetrack in North America has been Del Mar, which is a dirt surface, but they're not dealing with very much variation in water. They also have invested in state-of-the-art equipment, rebuilt their track to exact geometry, and maintain the track with careful attention to the details" (see Case Study—p. 184).

Del Mar doesn't have torrential rains normally, located in Southern California, but Peterson says the track superintendent and managers are extremely conscientious about maintaining consistency.

"It is not uncommon for us to test the track material on that track every two weeks," Peterson says. "Dennis [Moore], one of the superintendents there, pulls the rail every day, and grades a couple of times a week, and every race day."

The track also is extremely consistent on the *curve transition*—the most critical point of a track.

"When the horse is changing leads, there is not only a shift of weight on the horse between legs, but there's also the potential to bump other horses," Peterson says. "Everything needs to be as consistent as possible to help the horse and rider be able to smoothly ride through that."

9.3 Keeneland maintenance crews work to make the dirt footing consistent despite unpredictable weather conditions.

TRACK BASE BASICS

If you're constructing a track from scratch, George McDermott says there are three types of bases available for East Coast-style tracks: stabilized soil, clay, or crushed limestone. "Stabilized soil is the natural ground already there. You stabilize that by either compaction, or they can cut cement into it like a highway."

Some start with clay that is compacted well, then the surface material is added to the top.

Harness racing often has a stabilized soil underneath—could be clay and soil cemented to harden—and 3 to 6 inches of crushed limestone on top. A racetrack will add the surface footing on top of this base. A West Coast track is similarly constructed, but with a substrate of clay on top of the base, then a deeper layer of surface material.

"The clay normally settles to the bottom of the surface mixture after you manipulate it, and the soil on top becomes more sandy and doesn't hold together," McDermott says. "So they'll either add more clay to the material on top, or pull some of the clay material from the substrate up to remix and bind the top material together so it forms properly and is less sandy."

The footing for a dirt track ideally comes from a local sand pit. Otherwise the costs will increase exponentially.

"Normally you start with sand pits near you, and then find out if the material will work for your racetrack," McDermott explains. "You'll go through labs and they'll give you lab results on the material. The general idea is to get soil locally and amend that soil either with straight sand, or clay, something to bring it to the level you want. Each racetrack has their own target value that works very well for them."

McDermott says there are just a handful of soil labs in the country that can give results usable for maintaining a track.

"That's going to at least give you a target value of what you need to do."

9.4 *Keeneland's raceway has a polytrack base underneath the dirt, which makes for a very stable base.*

CASE STUDY

KEENELAND

Keeneland is a historic non-profit racetrack located in Lexington, Kentucky. Jim Pendergest has been the Director of Racing Surfaces for the track since 2019, with decades of experience at the facility.

Each day at Keeneland has a schedule for maintenance, and it varies during racing versus off season. Pendergest says maintenance on the turf track takes more time than the dirt one.

"There are just so many things to do with it," Pendergest says. "You're growing grass, it's a living organism and it requires constant care. We're mowing it every other day, we're fertilizing, we're treating it for disease and treating it for weeds."

Keeneland is unique from some other tracks because it still has the polytrack base from having a polytrack in the early 2000s underneath the dirt.

"Polytrack drains, and synthetics are supposed to drain vertically," Pendergest says. "The water goes straight through the wax coated material, and you have to have a draining system for that. We had the draining system in there for the polytrack and we left it when we put the dirt back on—we just covered it with crushed limestone to make the base for the dirt track."

Pendergest says with drainage, asphalt, and limestone under the track's 6 inches of dirt, he feels it's the best base in the country.

"It's completely protected, and we never worry about the integrity of the base," Pendergest says. "Unless we have an earthquake, there's really nothing that's going to impact that base. There's no other track in the world that has this kind of drainage system."

The track also has a porous rubber paving around the inside rail and outside rail to help water escape horizontally.

"This helps keep the track from having washouts from really heavy rains, like most tracks would," Pendergest explains. "We don't lose much footing—it stays on the track."

Where the dirt meets the porous rubber paving gives maintenance crews a visual to make sure the

track is even and at the right elevation. The dirt has a 3-inch cushion, and the lower 3 inches are compacted to create a hard pan.

"When the horses go through the cushion, they need to hit something firm that they can spring off of to propel themselves into the next stride," says Pendergest. "That 3 inches cushions the impact as they land, and then they get to the hard pan and that allows them to propel themselves forward."

9.5 Keeneland Director of Racing Services Jim Pendergest uses a spreadsheet to keep tabs on the turf track shear and penetration, as well as moisture added.

The composition of dirt at Keeneland is 85 percent sand, 12 percent silt, and 3 percent clay, and that's the mix they strive to maintain.

To maintain Keeneland's tracks, the facility has excellent equipment, including a Caterpillar grader with a GPS to maintain the surface at exactly the slope and depth needed.

Maintaining the footing at Keeneland is a challenge with unpredictable winter weather, Pendergest admits.

"We can get ice storms, hail storms, we can get rain in the afternoon and then the temperature drops to 20 degrees," Pendergest says. "That's probably the biggest challenge, because you get all that water in the surface, and it makes it really difficult to keep it from freezing at night if you want to train the next morning."

To monitor the moisture in the surface, Pendergest tests the moisture content every day at 54 different locations. And on race days, his team takes moisture measurements between races as well.

"We use a lot of science on this track, and our turf track," he says. "We use that as a guide to when we need to add water in the afternoons, or between races."

The racing surface is tested in a laboratory twice a year, and the lab will use a biomechanical hoof tester on the track to make sure it is consistent.

"They use ground-penetrating radar to check the base as a secondary assurance that everything is good underneath," Pendergest says.

For the turf track, he uses a Going Stick to measure the shear and penetration. "That helps us know how soft or firm the turf track is. We put all of that info into spreadsheets and we look at it every day. We also monitor how much moisture we've got, and how much we put on it when we irrigate."

The track has a weather system to inform on temperatures and humidity, which is factored into maintenance.

The main goal for caring for the track is consistency, Pendergest says. "If you are walking in the dark, and you're on a sidewalk, and the sidewalk ends but you can't see that and you step down six inches, that's painful, or you can fall. Think about a horse going 35 miles an hour—he has to have consistent footing all the way around that track. He can't step off a ledge. So the most important thing on a racetrack is not whether it's firm or soft, it's that it's consistent all the way around."

Keeneland is a not-for-profit, and Pendergest considers the facility one of the most beautiful in the country.

"Keeneland has a beautiful grandstand paddock, but also a beautiful barn area—it's just amazing, and it's kept up so well here," he says. "The whole package is just, I think, better than any place else you can go."

Primer Notes for Caring for Track Surfaces

McDermott says many folks might be surprised by how much work goes into maintaining a track. In addition to watering overnight and harrowing before morning works, before the races begin, in between races, and at the end of the day, the track is also maintained during days off.

"On the days there's no racing, the track crew is fully engaged in grading the racetrack, manipulating it, keeping it good for the training in the morning, and then they work all afternoon and almost into the evening to get it right," he says.

Turf

For a turf surface, Peterson says two things are most important: *aeration* and *top dressing*.

9.6 During racing season, track crews spend 16 to 18 hours a day working on the footing.

- **Aeration** is punching holes in the turf to allow more oxygen to get to the roots to promote growth.

- **Top dressing** is usually pure sand with no silt and clay to keep the material from getting too high a percentage of organic material, which can cause it to compact.

Both of these help the turf grow and support better biomechanics for the horse's hoof and limbs. By helping to grow strong roots, the turf stays intact during propulsion and can provide an even surface for the horses to travel over.

Moisture content is also crucial for turf courses, just like dirt courses.

"Any variation in moisture content is not good for the grass, not good for the horses, not good for the rider," Peterson says. "In a way it's easier on turf because you have these little green indicator flags that say it's too wet or too dry."

Growing the grass on a turf track is a specialty in itself, but Peterson says the root system and irrigation are the most important parts.

"If you've got a good root system, you've got a great racetrack," he says. "If you can look at the root system and see that it is thick and consistent, it's perfect, and then you do whatever you need to do to the top to make it even."

9.7 Two important assignments for maintaining a turf track are aeration and top dressing.

EXPERT TIP

Keeneland uses the same piece of equipment to groom the surface of their track on the first pass, second pass, and third pass, and makes sure it is cutting at the same depth as the last step every time. However, they do work the track in different patterns.

"They cannot work the same pattern every day, because you're going to make low and high spots where you're doing to drop off sand," Jim Pendergest says. "Start in a different spot every day, and work it in a different pattern so you're not pulling sand in the same direction all the time."

Synthetic

For a track made with synthetic footing, compaction is an issue, because it can eventually lead to drainage problems. Contamination is also an issue.

"Manure can inhibit the drainage," Peterson warns. "Segregation of the material can occur. The wax can come off the sand. It will need to be mixed."

Dirt

For a dirt track, breaks to harrow after a certain number of horses are worked help set up and maintain the hard pan below the surface that supports the hoof during secondary impact and propulsion.

9.8 A & B *Tracks on the West Coast and in the Southwest employ a roller harrow as a standard piece of maintenance equipment. The roller harrow has a cylinder across the full width of the implement to control the depth of the teeth (A). Between every race, and during breaks in training, the track is harrowed and watered (B).*

For dirt, and synthetic tracks, too, Peterson says keeping the depth of the cushion layer consistent is critical. This requires using a motor grader. How frequently, depends on the usage.

"You need to pull the material from underneath the rail daily," he emphasizes. "One of the reasons you need to pull from the rail is because the track slopes to the inside rail so the water runs off the top surface. You have to slope. What happens with use is the inside harrow teeth begin to build up material. The sand keeps moving downhill because of gravity. If you're not careful, the harrow can ride up on the mound of dirt developing on the inside edge of the track and dig into it. It's not good—not good for the horses because they're running on different surfaces without the same depth of cushion."

The goal for caring for a track is to keep the depth of the cushion perfectly consistent all the way across the track, Peterson says. That inside rail builds up dirt every day, depending on the composition of the track and its usage.

Moisture

Moisture management is a vital element to keeping a track's surface consistent and safe.

"Water trucks are the most important piece of equipment you've got at a racetrack," Peterson says. "Moisture control is the most difficult and the most important characteristic of a dirt or turf track."

Unlike arenas, irrigation and sprinklers do not work as a moisture management system for a dirt track.

"You have no idea how much water is going on these tracks to keep them intact and consistent," Peterson says.

Water gets applied overnight, and it is a key to the track being the right consistency for morning workouts. Moisture content is then measured throughout the track, at set times of day.

"If you asked me what was the moisture content at 10 a.m. on the third of February for one of the tracks that participate in our system, I would say, 'Give me a minute.' I would type it in, I'd open up the log, and I could tell you not only how much moisture was on that track, I could tell you the moisture content at the quarter pole versus the three-quarter pole to make sure they were getting consistent where they pull onto the track," Peterson says. "And that's the future of racing, to me. We're getting better because we take a different approach to health and welfare of the horse and rider. I see a time in the future where you will be able to ask what the quarter pole looked like after the fourth race, and I will be able to tell you."

EXPERT TIP

Before a rainstorm, crews will "float" the track surface with a flat plate taken across the footing so that water will run off without soaking in.

Exercise Tracks

If you have an exercise track on your property, or you wish to add one and then maintain it, Peterson says you want to make sure you have the correct equipment to care for it.

"It's just paying attention, but you have to have the equipment to help the surface recover and get those layers put together properly," he says.

For those training racehorses, don't make any huge changes to the composition, versus where your horses might be running, Peterson warns. Your goal at home is to keep the surface as close to the one at the track as possible.

"If you've got a training track in upstate New York, and the horses are going to be running at Saratoga, then you need to know what the footing is like at Saratoga and try to match it," Peterson says. "If you've got a farm in California and you'll be shipping to Santa Anita, you have to match Santa Anita."

Horses can adapt to a surface, but they can't adapt between strides, he explains. "The less they have to adapt, the better."

TRACK BUILDING TAKEAWAYS

If you're building a track at home, the most challenging thing is finding a flat area with water available—but where rain and groundwater run away from.

"The site planning is absolutely critical, and it can have a staggeringly large effect on the cost of the project," Peterson says. "You start moving large quantities of dirt, even for a ¾-mile training track 30 feet wide, that's a big area. Moving material is a huge expense."

Drainage needs to be considered and incorporated into your plan. Poor drainage or water flowing over the track will increase maintenance time and effort considerably.

Building a track takes months of construction, and a lot of investment, McDermott says. He suggests working with a consultant and an engineer who understand and have worked on racetracks, while McDermott cautions against hiring a road builder to build a track.

"I have had some of the best road people I know recommend soils, and it was totally wrong for a track," he says. "So you have to be careful with that."

Testing and Managing Track Wear and Weather Impacts

Some tracks replace their footing every year. Others, like Churchill Downs, have rarely been replaced.

"Churchill Downs has not replaced their surface since World War II, and has what is pretty much considered a great dirt surface," Peterson says. "And then you have Mountaineer [Racetrack, in West Virginia] and they replace it every year."

When a surface has a low quartz content—like Mountaineer—the sand will wear out, Peterson explains. It will break down pretty quickly. "Sand quality varies dramatically around the country. In California, almost regardless of price, the quality of the sand is relatively low. You cannot get high-quality sand with a high quartz content. In general, sand with a higher quartz content will be more durable."

California tracks do a series of tests every three to four weeks to check the composition and then add a small amount of sand to keep the particle size consistent. Once a year, they then have to take the material off to maintain the target grades because so much material has accumulated.

"It breaks down that quickly," Peterson says.

In Central Kentucky, Peterson notes that you can get sand that is over 97 percent quartz. High-quality sand in that area is abundant. The Belmont Park training track in New York experiences a lot of traffic from horses each day. So much that Peterson tests it three or four times a year.

"We test it because the sand is such high quality that it will hold up even through heavy use, it doesn't usually need to be replenished, even though fine material may have been lost when rain runs off the surface."

Regular testing of a track surface's composition is an important part of maintaining a track, Peterson says.

"Generally it's not necessary to replace the sand," Peterson says. "You have to supplement it, and set targets for the maintenance of it, and you need to do that on a very regular basis. And if it's a lower quality sand, that testing needs to be done every three or four weeks because it breaks down that quickly. If you have high quality sand, you might see a bit of variation—maybe two or three months will help you stay ahead of the game."

A track like Santa Anita Park outside Los Angeles, California, has 150 timed workouts every morning, 1,000 horses on a surface in a day.

"They actually have three maintenance breaks during training in the morning," Peterson says. "The numbers are just staggering."

RATING TRACK CONDITIONS

When you're betting on racehorses, knowing the condition of the track can be valuable information, but it's not so easily categorized as you might think. Ratings can also be helpful for riders to know the conditions of the dirt on which they'll be racing, and Peterson says there are many variables.

The temperature of a synthetic track is just as important as the moisture content on a dirt track, he says. "If you've got a horse that likes a slow, deep track, loves a good struggle, if you are on a hot day, that horse is going to perform just as well on a synthetic track as he would on a sloppy, sloe (slow) dirt track."

However, a track is categorized as "sloppy" in New York, it's not the same as "sloppy" in New Mexico. The composition of the footing—how much silt and clay versus sand—and the humidity are also factors.

"These ratings are completely dependent on the track you are at, and the expectations of the people who are there," Peterson says. "The difference between sloppy in New Orleans and sloppy at Remington Park [Oklahoma City, Oklahoma] are night and day, because the expectations are different. And they can both get sloppy."

McDermott agrees—the categories are debatable. Conditions are not consistent because the officials rating the track might rate it "muddy" initially, for example. But by the time horses race, it could have dried up and become "fast" or "good." McDermott says sometimes it can be hard to tell the condition of the track until the first race of the day. But here are the basics:

Fast: Dry, even surface. This is a "normal" day's conditions, with optimum moisture content. ("The times that horses have run there in the past couple of years dictate what 'fast' is," McDermott says.)

Muddy: Track holding water, making the surface heavier, with slower times.

Sloppy: Track wet on the surface and splashing, with times off during rain or after rain. It is still fair footing, but the times are off.

Wet Fast: The track has surface water on it but the base it still solid. Usually after a short, fast rain prior to the track being sloppy. This only lasts a short time before the track either dries, or gets sloppy or muddy.

Good: A track that is almost "fast." This means the footing is "Okay," McDermott says. "Not fast or slow."

Slow: A track that is wet both on the surface and the base. This happens when a track goes from muddy to deep and heavy, making times very slow.

Freezing Temperatures

Hard winters where the ground freezes and thaws a lot is tough on a track. In the winter, if the nighttime temperature drops below 28 degrees, the footing will freeze. The track crew will need to manipulate the ground all night to keep it loose for racing the next day.

"Otherwise, it'll freeze solid and it'll be like a rock," McDermott says. "You have to adjust to the climate that you have.

Rainfall

A wet track is fine, especially if the surface was properly "floated" before so most of the water runs off. But slow rain can permeate down through the surface.

"It's not so much how much rain you get, but how many minutes of rain you get," he explains. "If you have a slow, soft rain, it's much harder to work with than a hard, fast rain. They're great for growing grass, not so easy on a dirt track."

McDermott says track crews pay close attention to weather reports and radars to prepare for potential rainstorms.

"If you can manipulate the track to seal it off in time, then when water hits it, it'll run off and you'll be in good shape," McDermott says. "But if you miss it—and I've missed it several times—and it rains on you, that track can get sloppy."

If the material is good, McDermott says it'll dry out pretty quickly but will take more manipulation to get back to a safe condition."

Adding Water

When the temperatures skyrocket and the air is dry, you'll need a hefty amount of water to maintain a track.

"You can put 100,000 gallons of water on a racetrack a day," McDermott says.

CASE STUDY

DEL MAR RACETRACK

Del Mar Racing is located in Del Mar, California, near the Pacific Ocean. This makes the track both unique and a challenge to maintain.

"We have a lot of variables with humidity and wind and sun," Assistant track manager Steve Wood says. "It doesn't matter what your weather conditions are—we're right on the ocean. I can hear the waves—they're breaking right now. That's how close to the ocean we are."

Wood says being located in California, Del Mar is surrounded by folks who are both for and against racing, so the track operates under a microscope.

"We have some of the best trainers and horses in the world here," Wood says. "For the last four years, we have been the safest track in the country. And I think we're probably one of the only tracks that laser and grade the track weekly."

This ensures that the banking going into the turns and straightaways are all the same.

9.9 Del Mar has a reputation for being the safest track in the country, and Wood attributes that in part to conscientious maintenance.

9.10 Lasered and graded weekly, Del Mar footing is extremely consistent, despite being located so close to the ocean.

9.11 *Del Mar's track is on the cutting edge of track and racing surfaces.*

"If your grade is off, then everything else will be off," Wood says. "If your cushion is not consistent across the whole track, meaning instead of a 10-inch profile everywhere, it's 11 here, nine here, 10 there, it makes everything different. It makes the water act differently in those locations. When the horse hits the ground, that shock comes back up to his hoof. So, if you have everything consistent at all times, then you ensure the safety and longevity of the horse."

California has implemented strict protocols about tracks, veterinarians, and medications. And Wood feels the state is on the cutting edge of track and racing surfaces.

Del Mar's track has a 10-inch profile and Wood works the top 5½ to 6 inches daily, maintaining a 3¼-inch cushion. The surface is made of 14.5 percent silt and clay with sand.

"You're setting up a pad, almost like a buffer as a horse hits it, like a dampening, it slowly stops him but absorbs the shock," explains Wood.

Wood works with Del Mar track superintendent Dennis Moore to maintain Del Mar, spending 16 to 18 hours a day on it during racing season.

"I've worked horse shows, I've done dressage, I've done jumpers, I've worked at Del Mar Horse Park. But nothing is as important or as crucial as a racetrack," Wood says. "An eighth of an inch of difference changes everything."

This involves evaluating soil samples, looking at the weather each hour, the wind, and the track's schedule so they can ensure a safe surface for today and tomorrow.

"Equipment and even different driving speeds change the way the implement goes on the ground, and can change the running or racing for the day. We know we have not just a horse, but a human on top of that horse, and a life and a family. So we know we have to ensure the safety of the horse and also the rider."

SOURCE NOTES AND COMMENTARY

Along with the in-depth interviews with the contributors listed at the beginning of this book (see p. xi), I referred to two resources in the course of my research, both made available to the public by the Fédération Equestre Internationale (FEI) and available at inside.fei.org:

Equine Surfaces White Paper. 2014. Authors: Sarah Jane Hobbs, Ph.D., University of Central Lancashire, UK, Alison J. Northrop, M.Sc., Anglia Ruskin University, UK, Christie Mahaffey, Ph.D., Racing Surfaces Testing Laboratory, USA, Jaime H. Martin, Ph.D., Myerscough College, UK, Hilary M. Clayton, BVMS, Ph.D., MRCVS, Michigan State University, USA, Rachel Murray, MA VetMB MS Ph.D., MRCVS, Animal Health Trust, UK, Lars Roepstorff, DVM, Ph.D., Swedish University of Agricultural Sciences, Sweden, Michael "Mick" Peterson, Ph.D., University of Maine, USA

—Since 2009, the FEI has supported research into the effect of arena surfaces on the orthopedic health of sport horses. This white paper is a collection of published scientific papers and data and is considered a work in progress.

Equestrian Surfaces—A Guide. 2014. Authors: Elin Helmlund, Cecelia Lönnell, Carolyne A Tranquille, Lars Roepstorff, Rachel C Murray, Hilary Clayton, Michael Peterson, Jaime Martin

—A joint venture between the Swedish Equestrian Federation and the Swedish University of Agricultural Sciences.

Below are additional notes related to information included in the pages of this book. Please refer to "Equine Surfaces" and *Equestrian Surfaces—A Guide* for more detailed information.

(Chapter 3)

—Consistency is crucial to a good arena surface. While a horse can adapt to a range of surfaces, the "Equine Surfaces" white paper says training on dramatically different surfaces may negatively impact performance, and can be associated with injury. There's a conundrum, though. Unlike surfaces designed for human athletics, an arena footing ideal for performance is not always ideal for long-term soundness, according to studies cited in the white paper.

—Barrey et. al. 1991 defines *shock absorption* as either frictional, where damping is achieved by the displacement of particles, or *structural*, where damping is achieved by the deformation of those viscoelastic particles. (Or: Impact firmness and cushioning determine how much a surface absorbs shock, or conversely, how rigid it is.)

—The resistance of a material against penetration with a defined object under a defined pressure (Nigg and Yeadon, 1987). This is a material property. It's difficult to measure accurately on arena surfaces. It is related to stiffness—the ratio of applied force to deflection.

—When a hoof impacts a surface, some of that energy from the collision is lost. The amount depends on the elasticity of the surface's top layer. A study by Setterbo et. al in 2011 cited in the "Equine Surfaces" white paper found that an "Ideal, safe surface should have a relatively low energy loss along with low hardness, which is difficult to achieve." A surface ideal for some uses might not be ideal for others.

—The moisture content of a footing is the largest variable to its consistency. But a variation in depth contributes the most to the risk of lameness, according to a study on dressage horses (Dyson, 2002) presented in the "Equine Surfaces" white paper.

—Dressage riders in the United Kingdom often use surfaces that are comprised of sand and rubber, sand, woodchip, and sand and polyvinylchloride (PVC), (Murray et al., 2010a). Additives for a dressage arena include synthetic or natural fibers, rubber, cloth or felt strips.

—A woodchip layer below the primary surface offers great cushioning, by reducing hardness, and increasing shock absorbency (Drevemo and Hjertén, 1991).

—When using woodchips as a primary source material, the "Equine Surfaces" white paper says there's an increase in the occurrence of slipping in the horse. As woodchip material degrades, it will become less cushioning and shock-absorbing.

—Less maintenance, no dust, more consistency across the surface, and a longer-lasting surface: A study by Murray et al., 2010a) found a wax-coated sand footing reduced incidence of lameness and injury versus sand and woodchip surfaces.

—A well-maintained fiber and sand arena can last for 20 years, says *Equestrian Surfaces*, but afterward it will be considered waste, and it will need to be disposed of properly, which can be expensive.

—In terms of equine surfaces, age is a significant factor in influencing leachate emissions (Birkholz et al, 2003). Newly produced (<6 months) rubber additives have higher levels of emissions than their older counterparts (Li et al, 2010). It may therefore be prudent to consider "ageing" the rubber additives in controlled conditions before integration into a surface mixture. Since local conditions and standards vary among countries, it would be prudent to control the drainage from any equine arena that contains rubber additives due to the evidence of pollution as described above.

(Chapter 5)

—Too much dust in an arena can contribute to inflammatory respiratory diseases (Pirie et al., 2003) and when a horse inhales too much dust, it can increase mucus in the trachea, reducing the availability of oxygen, and consequently, negatively impacting a horse's performance.

ACKNOWLEDGMENTS

A book of any kind takes a village to become a reality. And a book of this scope only happened with the help of many people! I have to start by thanking my Red River Writers Club. Kate, Chris, and Larri Jo: This is all your fault. But I couldn't have done it without you and our group text at each step of the process. I owe each of you a margarita.

I owe the greatest thanks to Bob Kiser, a man I hold in such high regard for his expertise, and after working together on this project, also for his kindness. Thank you for your generosity and for taking the time to help me make this the best book about arenas that I could possibly write. All I wanted for this book was to put some of your expertise on the page for horse folks, and I hope what we've written together is a worthwhile tribute to the inestimable contributions you have made to the horse world.

Also, thank you so much to Gwen MacKenzie, who coordinated all my correspondence with Bob.

Thank you to each and every source who carved out time from your busy schedules of building and maintaining arenas and tracks to share your knowledge with me. I'm so grateful for your assistance!

To every friend who has encouraged me in this quest to write a book about dirt, thank you! Your uplifting words have buoyed my spirits at challenging times. I am so thankful for y'all!

Thank you Rebecca and Martha at Trafalgar Square Books—I could not have asked for a more helpful publishing team. Thank you for making my goal of writing a comprehensive book like this a reality—only better, with your guidance.

Thank you to my parents, for indulging a horse-crazy little girl with riding lessons, horse magazine subscriptions, and a horse of my own. I cannot imagine where I'd be today if I hadn't fallen in love with horses and you allowed that dream to bloom. To my mom Cynde, and my grandma Sara, who instilled in me a deep love of reading books, I know you'd read this one too if you were still with us. To my dad, Cran, thank you for always cheering me on in everything I do.

To my husband, Zach, thank you for being my support so I could write this book. Thank you for making me coffee as I conducted countless 6:00 a.m. interviews with sources on other continents, and as I headed off to sunrise/sunset photo shoots of arenas. I have you to thank for keeping me sane and motivated. I love you so much.

To Wilder and Felicity, thank you for being the best kids in the world, and for believing in me. I hope you each chase after your dreams someday. If I can write a book, I know you can do anything!

Thank you to my Lord and savior, Jesus, for creating horses, and giving me the skills to write about them.

Finally, thank you to Diez, Wonder, Cowboy, Aaron, and most of all, Willy. You are the horses who have given me wings.

INDEX

Page numbers in *italics* indicate illustrations.

A

Active-Aqua system, 99, 106
Aeration, of turf, 177, *177*
Airflow, 45–46, *47*
All-around events, 23–24, 26, 140–141, *140*
Arenas
    care tips, 136–139 (*See also* Maintenance)
    design of (*See* Construction; Planning)
    lifespan of, 151, *152*
    myths regarding, 7
    size of, 12, *13*, 26–29, *28*, 45
    surface attributes, 1–3, 5, 52, 54–56 (*See also* Footing)
ArenaWet system, 99, 101, 105–106
Attwood, Nick, 3
Austin, Danny, 14

B

Bacher, Wolfgang, 14
Barrel racing
    design for, 23, 26, 39–40, 71, 73
    maintenance for, 110, 120, 129, 132, 144–145, *145*
Base layers
    construction of, 14, 20, 80–82, 84, 87, *89*, 127
    grading for, 7, 46, 74–78, *75*
    maintenance of, 136, 154–156
    for racetracks, 166–167, 172, 173
    troubleshooting, 102, 154–156, 160
Belmont Park, 181
Biomechanics, of stride, 5–6, *5*, 165–166
Builders, 33. *See also* Construction

C

Cannon, Sydney, 95
Card, Vinnie, 36, 40
Carpet fiber, 59, 60, 70
Cheyenne Frontier Days, 150
Churchill Downs, 181
Clay, 58, 76, 96, 112, 153, 172
Climate, 20, 168. *See also* Site selection
Compaction, 78–79, 81, 84, *85*, 124, 178
Comparative weights moisture measure, 106–107, *107*
Competition arenas
    case studies, 34–40, 127, 132, 150
    footing in, 1, 102, 112
    maintenance of, 131, 133
    planning considerations, 24, 26, 36
Concrete
    for structure foundations/supports, 45, 87
    in/under surfaces, 54, 57, 127, 142, 146
Concussion, 52
Construction
    of footing layers, 74–77, *75*
    planning for, 9–33, 77–80, 82–88, *89*
    of racetracks, 167–168, 180
    WEC case study, 36–37
Consultants, 33, 90, 156
Containment structures, for footing, 30, 79, 81, 82
Contaminants, 20, 70, 134, 137–139
Contractors, 90–92. *See also* Construction
Cost considerations, 49, 51, 69, 81
Covered arenas
    construction of, 27, *27*, 30–33, 86–88, *88–89*
    design considerations, 15, 41–51, *43*, *47*
Cow horse events, 23, 30, 73, 110, 112, 142
Cupolas, 46
Curve transition, in racing, 171
Cushioning, 55
Cutting events, 71, 73, 112, 131, 142–144, *143*

D

Del Mar Racetrack, *167*, 184–187, *184–186*
Detweiler, David, 115–116
Dirt surfaces. *See* Natural material footing
Disc roto tillers, 124
Disciplines, design/maintenance for, *25*, 26, 138–145. *See also specific disciplines*
Dragging
    construction planning for, 29
    equipment, 115, 117–120, *117–119*, 125, 163
    moisture management and, 96, 114
    patterns in, 129–131, *130*, 157, 163
    of racetracks, 177
    tips for, 93, 129, 133–134, 159
Drainage
    construction for, 77, 78, 79, 80
    for indoor vs. outdoor arenas, 44, 46, 87
    planning for, 14, 15, 17, 86, 150
    for racetracks, 168–169, 173, 180
    repair considerations, 154–156

for round pens, 18–19
slope in, 7, 78, 84, 105, 106, 160, 179
systems for, 7, 76, 99, 105, 155
Dressage
design for, 23, 26, 27–29, *28*, 32
footing for, 55–56, 139
Drum rollers, 123–124
Dust, 58, 62, 64, 95, 110, 137–138, 149

E

Easy Flow drainage pipe, 155
Ebb and Flow drainage system, 76, 99, 105
Energy loss (surface attribute), 54
English arenas
design/construction of, 26, 77–80, 82, 88
footing materials, 55–56, *56*, 77
maintenance of, 110, 133
Equestrian Surfaces, a Guide (Swedish Equestrian Federation), 5–6
Equine Surfaces White Paper, 3, 46, 52, 54–56
Equipment
key types, 117–125, 163
planning for, 29
selection of, 19, 115–117, *116*
storage/maintenance of, 125–126, 138
Evaporation, 82, 98–99, 101, 105–106, 114, 131, 133
Eventing, 23
Exercise tracks, 180

F

Fabric. *See also* Textile fibers, in footing
for arena structures, 45
as underlayment, 80, 86
Facilities, generally, 17–18, 37, 45, 78, 87
Fans, 32, 44, 46
Felt, 60–62, *61*, *63*, 69, 80
Fencing, 30–31, *31*, *48*, 49–50, 84, 86, 88
Fiber, in footing, 60–62, *61*, *63*, 69, 70, 136

Field Scout moisture meter, 107–109, *108*
Firmness, of footing, 54–55, 93, 127, 153
"Floating" of surfaces, 95, 179, 183
Flooding, 95, 97
Footing
overview, 1–5, *2*, *4*, 52, 70–71
analysis of, 69–70, 149, 153, 156, 160–162, 175, 181
attributes of, 24, 26, 52–56, 93–94
blending, 66–69, *67–68*, 148
consistency of, 54, 55, 93, 118–119, 175
construction and, 12, 14, 30, 79, 81, 82
disposal of, 65
installation of, 80–81, 86, 88
longevity of, 44, 94
materials for, 56–66, *56*, *63*, 69–70, 77
measurement of, 160–161
myths regarding, 7
selection of, 23–24, *25*, 46
troubleshooting, 151, 153–154, 157–159
WEC case study, 38–40, *39*
Freezing
footing and, 46, 98, 168, 175, 183
of watering systems, 100–101, 114, 126
French drains, 155

G

Gates, 29, 79
Geotextile membranes, 74, *75*, 76
Grading. *See also* Base layers
for construction, 78, 81, 84, 87, 90–91
of racetracks, 184, 187
re-leveling/repair, 136, 157, 160
Grass surfaces, 1, 52, *53*, 64–66, 168–169
Grip, of footing, 23, 55, 60, 93, 127
Grooming. *See* Maintenance

H

Halter classes, 145

Hand test moisture measure, 109–110, *109*
Hand tools, 22, 124, 128, 157
Hand-watering, 97–98, 100
Hard surfaces, 5. *See also* Firmness, of footing
Harness racing, 172
Harrows and harrowing, 125, 166, 178–179, *178*
Hold, defined, 23
Holes, 66, 73, 129, *141*, 144, 154, 157
Hoof-surface interaction, 5–6, *5*
Hot walker spaces, 19
Hydraulics, 123, 126

I

Impact firmness, 54–55
Indoor arenas, 15, 41–51, *43*, *47*, 86–88, *88–89*
Injuries
prevention of, 1, 3, *4*, 6, 8, 132
risk factors, 3, 5, 59, 95, 169

J

Jumping
design for, 23, 26, 29, 40, 45
footing for, 55–56, 64, 110, *135*, 139–140, *139*

K

Keeneland racetrack, *170*, *172*, 173–175, *174*, 177
Kick walls/kickboards, 30–31, *31*
Kiser, Bob, 1, 71–73

L

Lazy E Arena, 132
Leveling, of footing surface, 118–119, 125, 160. *See also* Grading
Lighting, 31–32, *32*, 38, 42, 48, *48*
Loam, 20, 58

Location. *See* Site selection
Longeing, 138

M

Magnesium chloride, 113
Maintenance. *See also* Equipment; Moisture management
   overview, 7, 127–133
   case studies, 40, 174–175
   of drainage pipe systems, 76
   footing type and, 60–61, 62
   moisture management as, 93–97
   myths regarding, 7
   planning for, 29, 42–44, *43*, 46, 158–162
   of racetracks, 176–179
   vs. repair, 156
   tips for, 133–134, 136, 157–158
Manure management, 60, 124, 137–138, *137*, 144, 178
Materials, sourcing, 14–15, 66, *68*, 69–70, 91, 172
McDermott, George, 164
Membranes, 74, *75*, 76, 80, 86
Metal materials, 45, 49
Middle layers, 77
Mirrors, 32
Moisture management
   overview, 93–97, *94*, 131, 133
   additives for, 113
   assessments for, 106–110, *107–109*, 162
   climate and, 101, 113, 114
   for competition arenas, 133, 146–150
   by discipline, 110–112
   for racetracks, 171, 175, 177, 179, 182, 183
   routines/systems for, 12, 44, 79, 96–106, 114
   for turf, 177
Moore, Dennis, 171, 187
Mountaineer Racetrack, 181
Mud, 58, 87
Music systems, 32

N

Natural material footing. *See also* Sand
   maintenance of, 116–117, 118
   quality of, 69, 151, 153
   for racetracks, 169–171, *170*, 172–174, 178–179, *178*
   soil types in, 17, 58, 71, 73

O

Observation, in arena maintenance, 110, 128, 159
Oklahoma City Fairgrounds, 127
Organic material, 20, 22, 134, 138, 159, 177
Outdoor arenas
   construction of, 77–80, 82–86, *83*, *85*
   design considerations, 7, 15, 17, 41–51, *43*, 58
   WEC case study, 40
Owners, responsibilities of, 92

P

Pad preparation, 78–79, 82–84, *83*, 87. *See also* Grading
Pendergest, Jim, 168, 173
Perimeter barriers, 30–31, *31*, 79. *See also* Fencing
Peterson, Mick, 164
Planning
   overview, 9–10, *11*, 33
   arena size and, 26–29, *28*
   budget considerations, 10, 12–15, *13*
   exercise tracks, 180
   fencing and barriers, 30–31, *31*
   lighting, 31–32, *32*
   site selection, 15–22, *16*, *21*
   use considerations, 23–26, *25*
   WEC case study, 34, 36
Polo, 64
Polymer coatings, 62. *See also* Waxed sand surfaces
Proctor tests, 106, *107*
Property location. *See* Site selection
Purchase (surface attribute), 110. *See also* Grip

R

Racetracks
   case studies, 173–175, 184–187
   construction of, 167–168
   maintenance of, 176–179, 181–183, 184
   safety considerations, 164, *165*
   track condition ratings, 182
Rainwater, 97, 98, 123–124, 150, 154, 183
Rebound, 23, 93–94
Reining
   design for, 23, 26, 30, 32, 39–40, 71, 73
   footing for, 110, 112, *134*, 138, 141–142, *141*
Repair work, 151–159
Repetitive maneuvers, holes from, 65, 71, 137–138
Respiratory health, 95
Responsibilities, of owners, 92
Responsiveness, of footing, 54–55, 93, 127
Rider feedback, 156, 159
Ridge vents, 46
Ripper blades, 86, 87, 112, 119, *119*, 120, 125
Roberts, Roby, 34, 37
Roberts family, 34
Rocks, 69, 76, 81, 139, 155
Rodeo events, 73, 132, 146–150, *147*
Rollover, biomechanical, *5*, 6
Round pens, *13*, 18–19, *19*, 100
Rubber, as footing material, 58–59

S

Safety considerations
    arena design for, 1, 31, 37–38, 127
    owner responsibility and, 92
    for racetracks, 164, 184, 187
Sand
    coated, 56, 62, 64, 101
    moisture management with, 76–77, 93–94, 96, 112
    qualities of, 56–58, 82, 151, 153–154, 161–162, 181
    on racetracks, 168
    textile fibers with, 60–62, *61*, *63*
Sandy loam, 20, 58
Santa Anita Park, 181
Sawdust, in footing, 59–60
Screenings (base material), 81
Shadows, 38, 42
Shear strength, 54
Sheet water flow, 20, *21*
Shock absorption, 54
Shovel work, 22, 124, 128, 157
Shows. *See* Competition arenas
Sieve analysis, 66, *67–68*
Silt, 58, 76, 154
Site selection, 14–22, *16*, *21*, 78, 180
Skylights, 44
Sliding stops, 65, 71
Slope, in drainage, 7, 78, 84, 105, 106, 160, 179
Smith, Leland, 26, 73, 132
Snodgress, Randy, 7, 69
Spectators, 33
Spinning maneuvers, 138
Sprinkler systems, 12, 98, 100–101, 157–158, 162
Stability, of footing, 94
Stock horse arena formula, 71–73
Stone dust, 81. *See also* Rocks
Stride, phases of, 5–6, *5*, 165–167
Surfaces, for racetracks, 168–171. *See also* Footing
Synthetic footing. *See also* Textile fibers, in footing
    maintenance of, 117, 120, 131, 133
    for racetracks, 169, 178, 182

T

Textile fibers, in footing
    maintenance considerations, 82, 151, 153, 162
    qualities of, 60–62, *61*, *63*
    sources for, 69, 70
Top dressing, of turf, 177, *177*
Top layers, *75*, 77, 80–82, 86, 88, 166
Topsoil, 22, 78, 81, *83*, 84
Tractors, 82, 121–123, *122*, 125–126, 138–139
Trailers, for watering, 99, 102–104, *103*, 120–121, 126
Training arenas, 24, 26
Training tracks, 24, 180
Trenches, 79
Trucks, for watering, 98, 101–102, 120–121, 179
Turf racetracks, 168–169, 173, 175, 176–177
Turnout, avoiding, 136–137
Tying, of horses, 137

U

Underground watering systems, 99, 104–106

V

Vegetable oil, as sand coating, 64
Ventilation, 45–46, *47*
Viewing areas, 33

W

Walls, 30–31. *See also* Fencing
Water flow patterns, 20, *21*, 22. *See also* Drainage; Moisture management
Waxed sand surfaces, 56, 62, 64, 101
Weather, 20, 46, 95, 97, 168, 184. *See also* Freezing
Western arenas
    case studies, 40, 132
    design/construction of, 23, 26, 29–30, 82–88, *83*, *85*
    footing materials, 56, 71–73, *72*
    maintenance of, 105, 110, 118, 129–131, *130*
Wetlands, 22
Wind, 32, 44, 46, 100, 101
Windows, 46
Wood, Steve, 184
Wood materials, 30, 45, 49, 59–60, 100, 138
World Equestrian Center, Ocala, 34–40, *35–36*, *38–39*